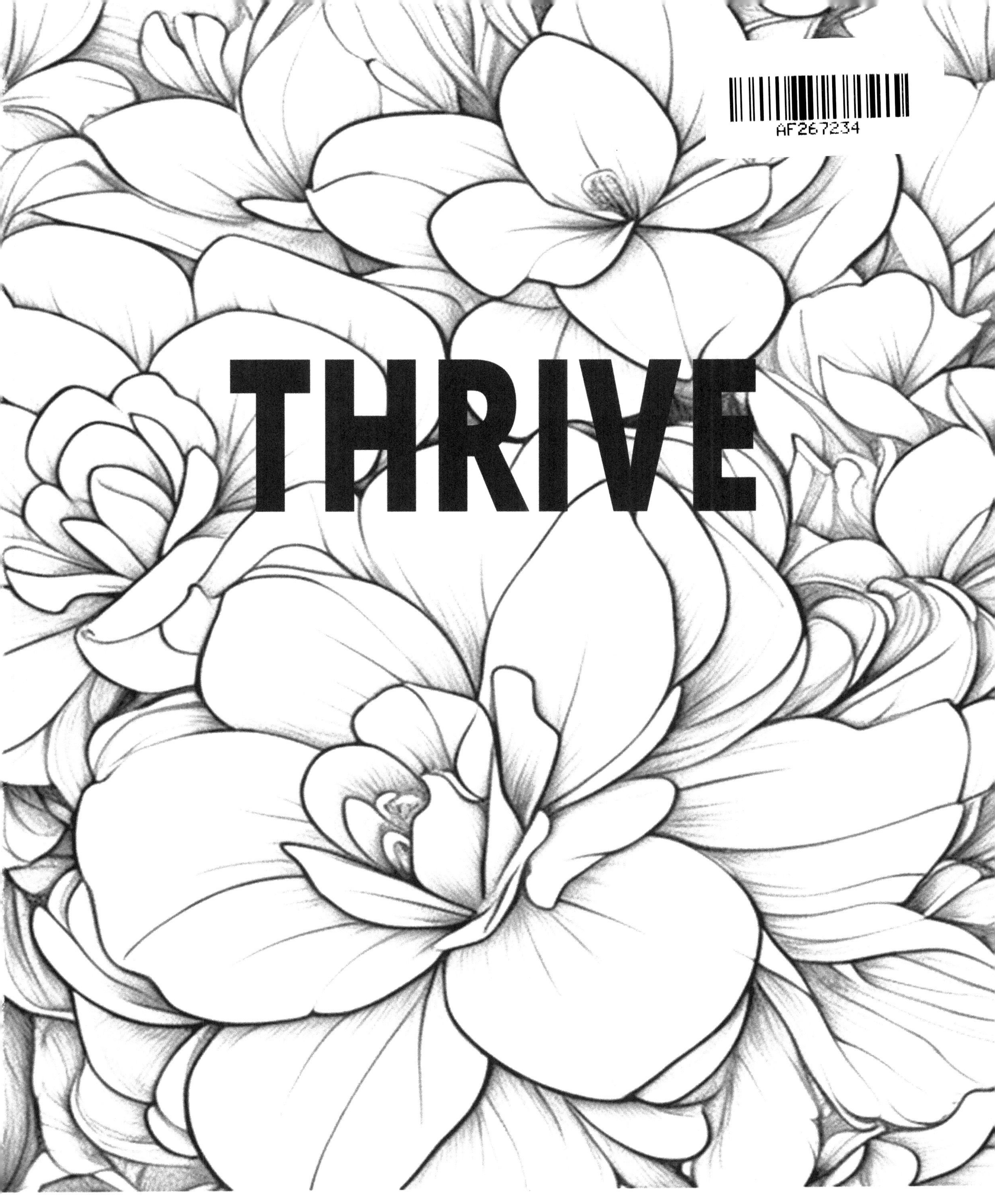
AF267234
THRIVE
PEARLSOFGREATPRICE.ORG

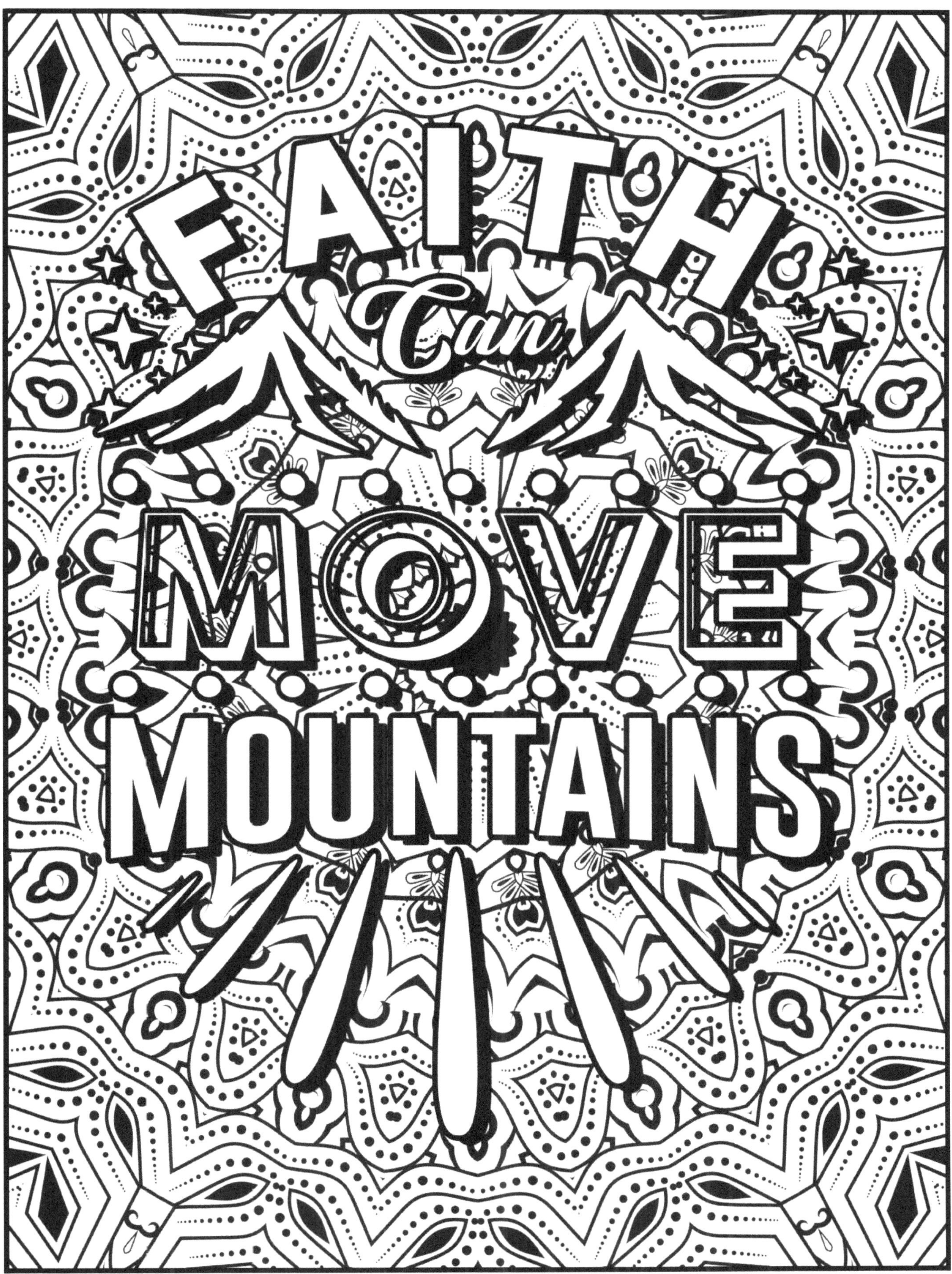

FAITH
Can
MOVE
MOUNTAINS

I CAN DO ALL THINGS THROUGH CHRIST WHO STRENGTHENS ME PHILIPPIANS 4:13

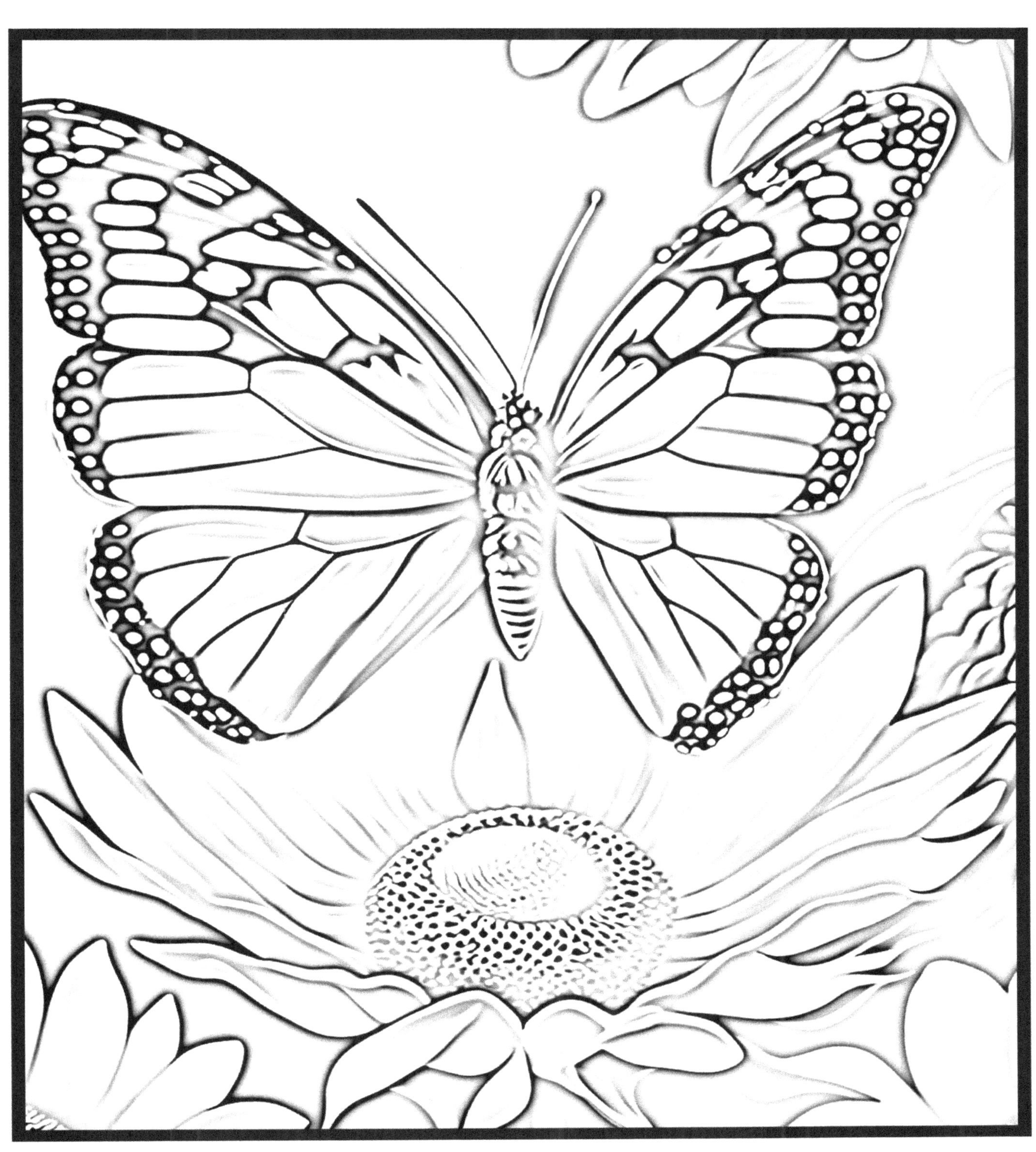

IF I GO TO THE DEPTHS, BEHOLD, YOU ARE THERE

PSALM 139:8

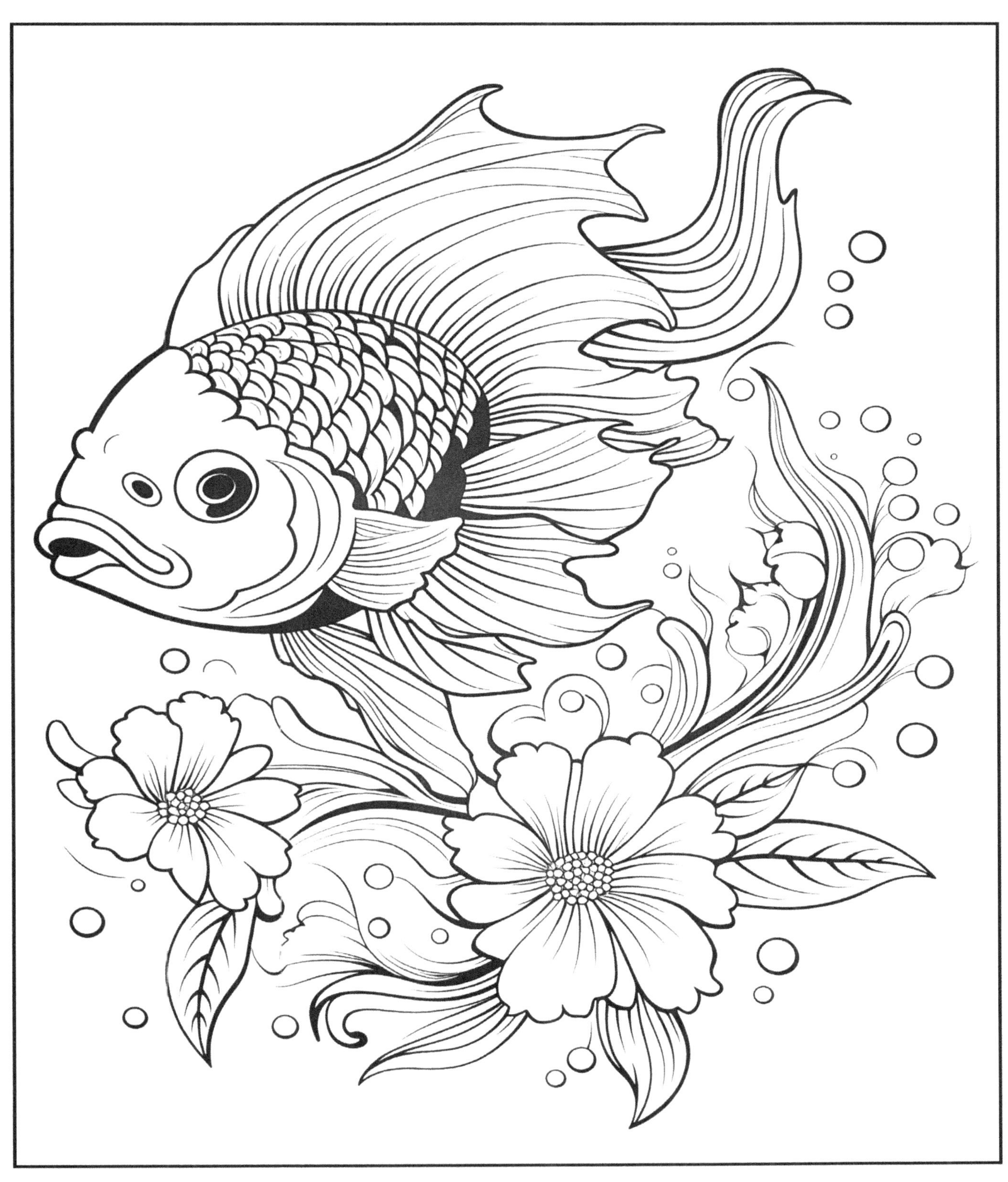

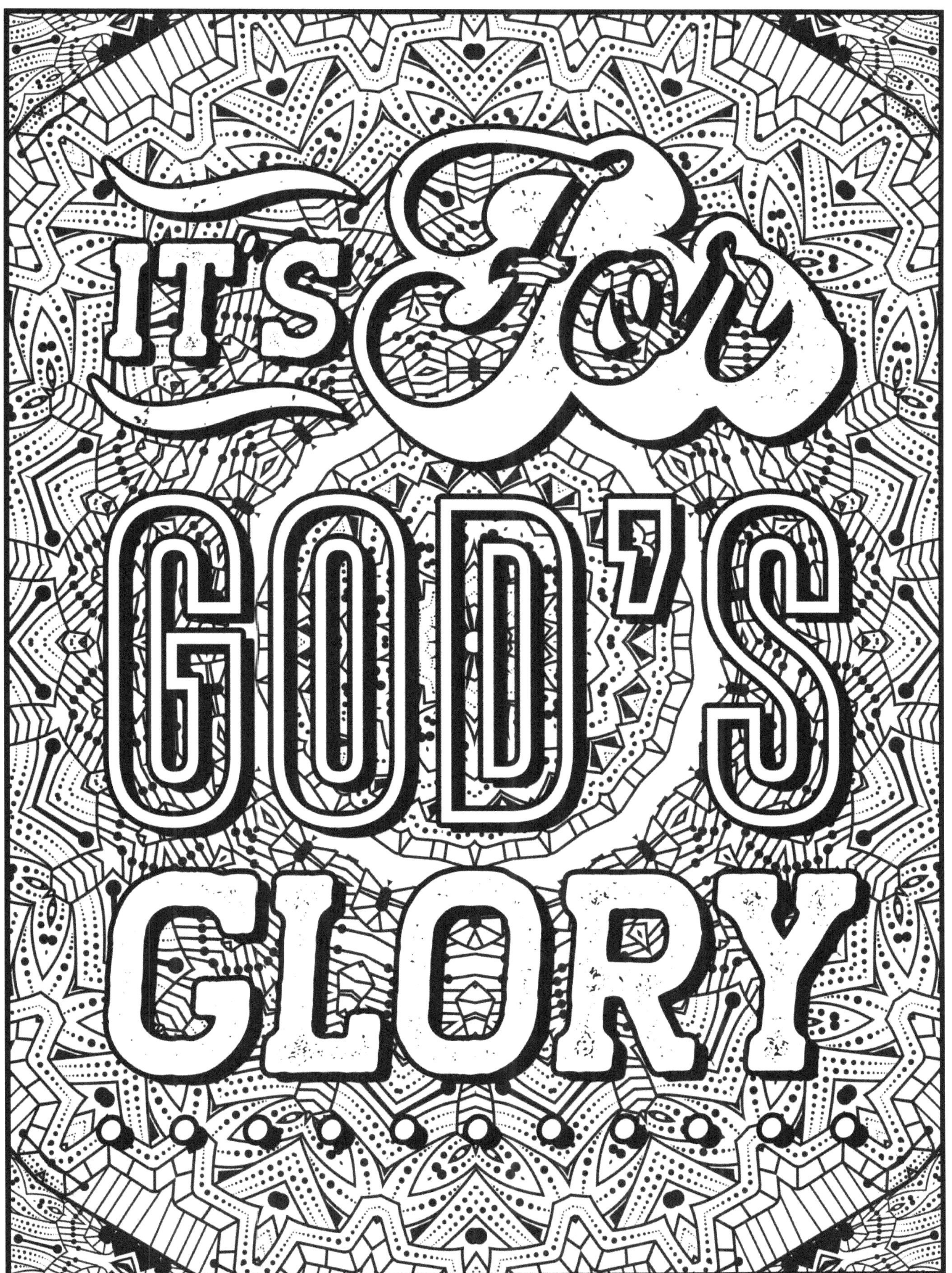

IT'S For
GOD'S
GLORY

GOD IS LOVE, WHOEVER LIVES IN LOVE, LIVES IN GOD

1 JOHN 4:16

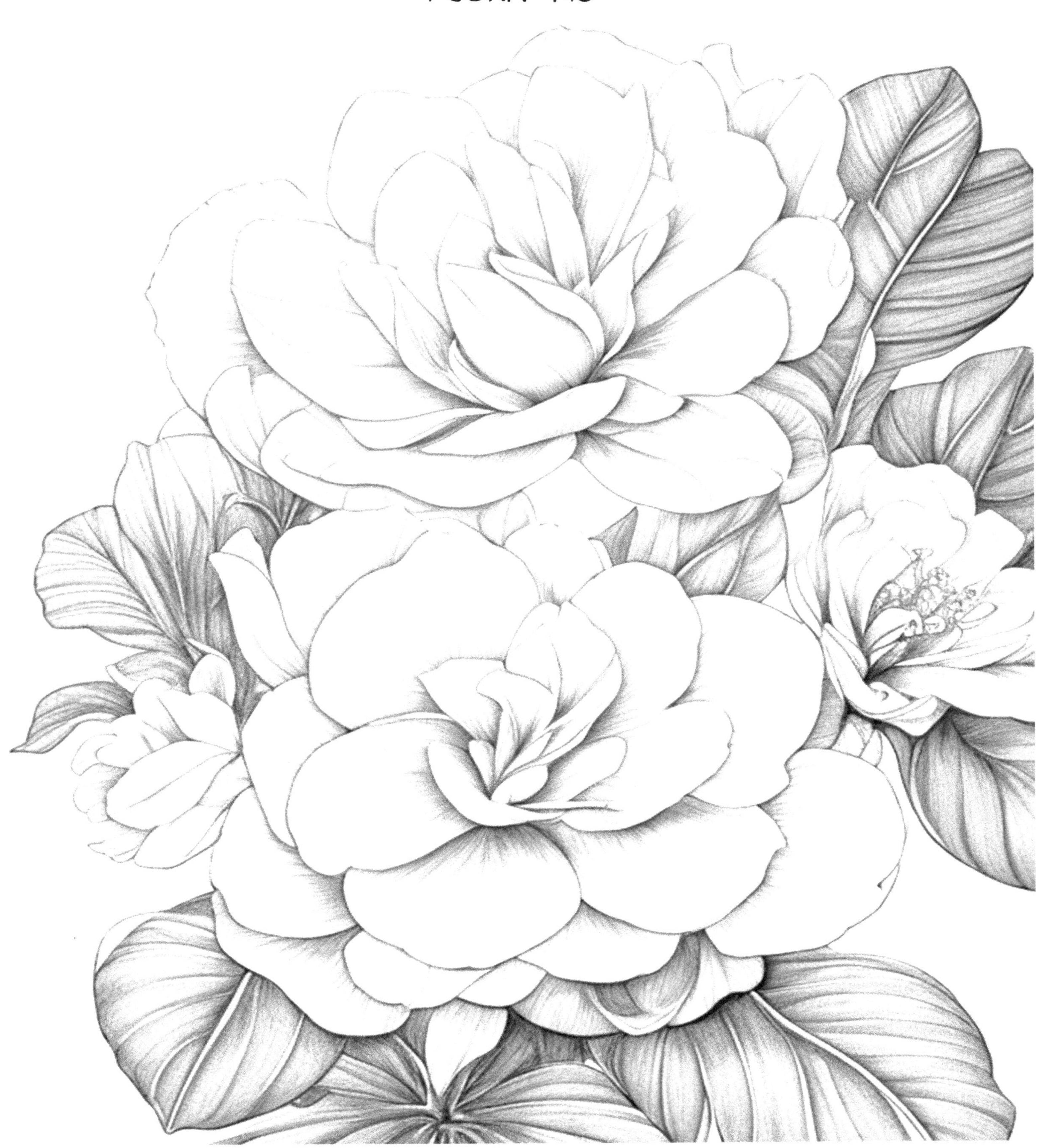

THE LORD WILL NEVER LEAVE YOU NOR FORSAKE YOU

DEUTERONOMY 31:6

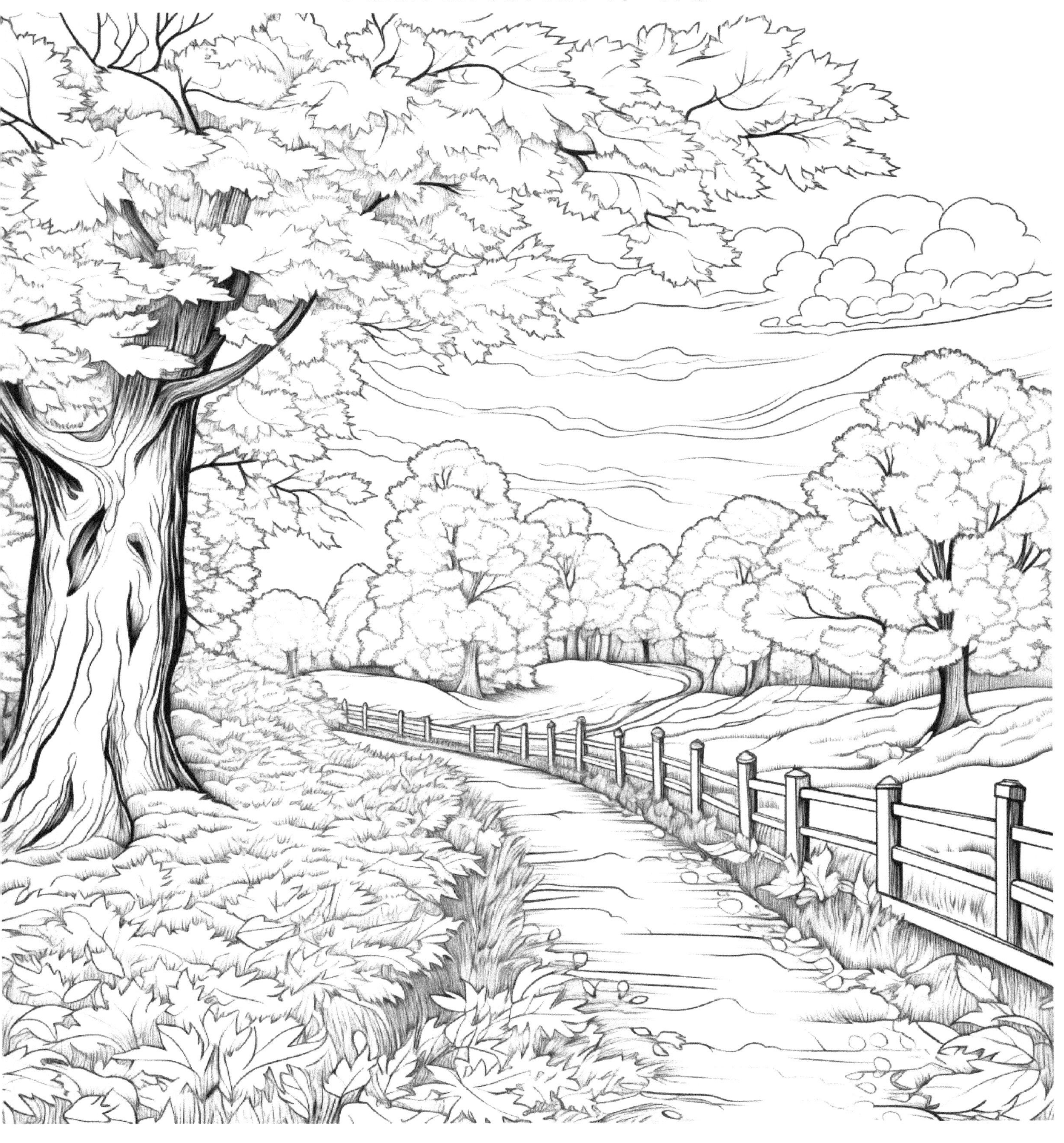

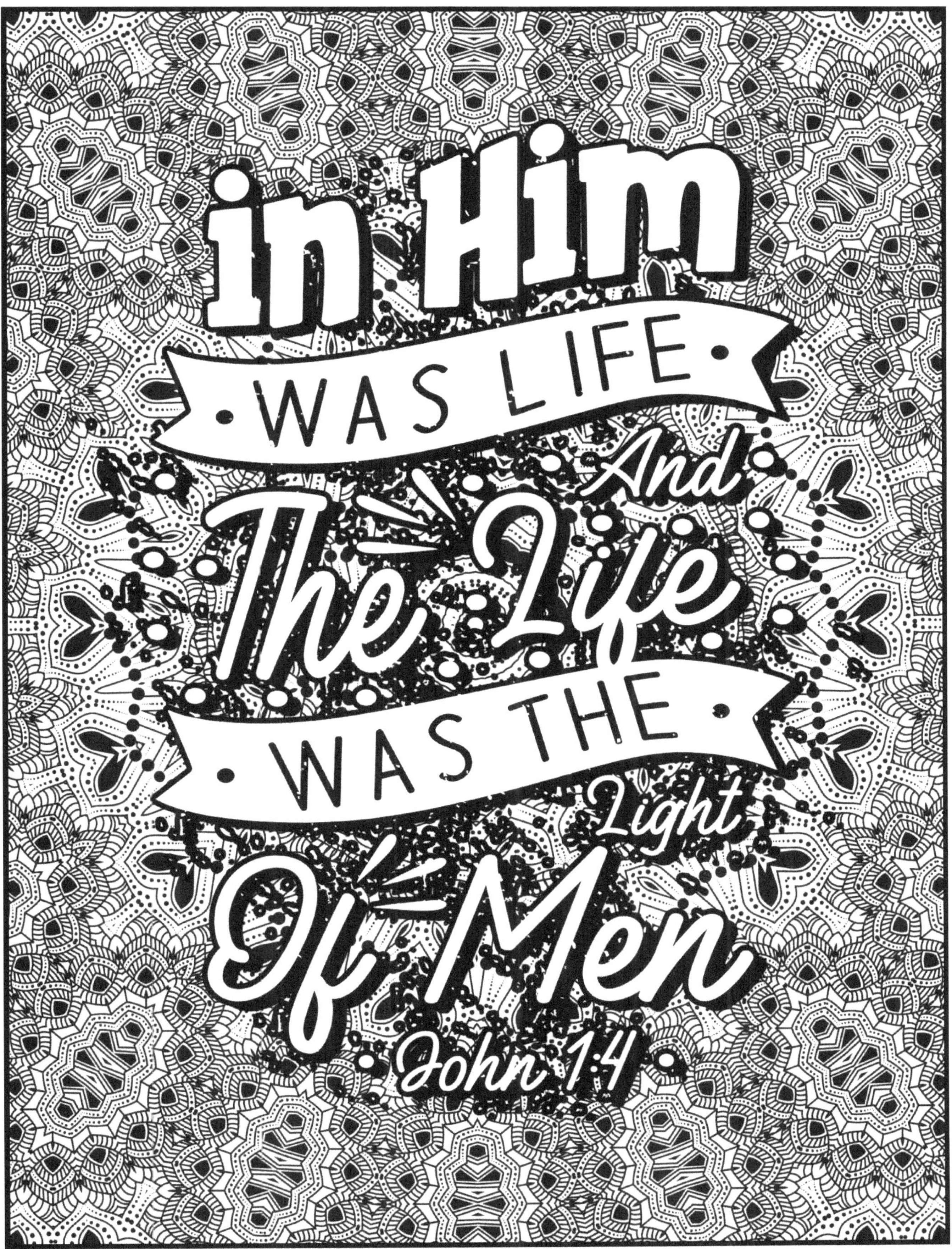

in Him
was life
And
The Life
was the
Light
Of Men
John 1:4

THE LORD IS MY SHEPHERD
I SHALL NOT WANT HE LEADS ME BESIDE STILL WATERS.

PSALM 23

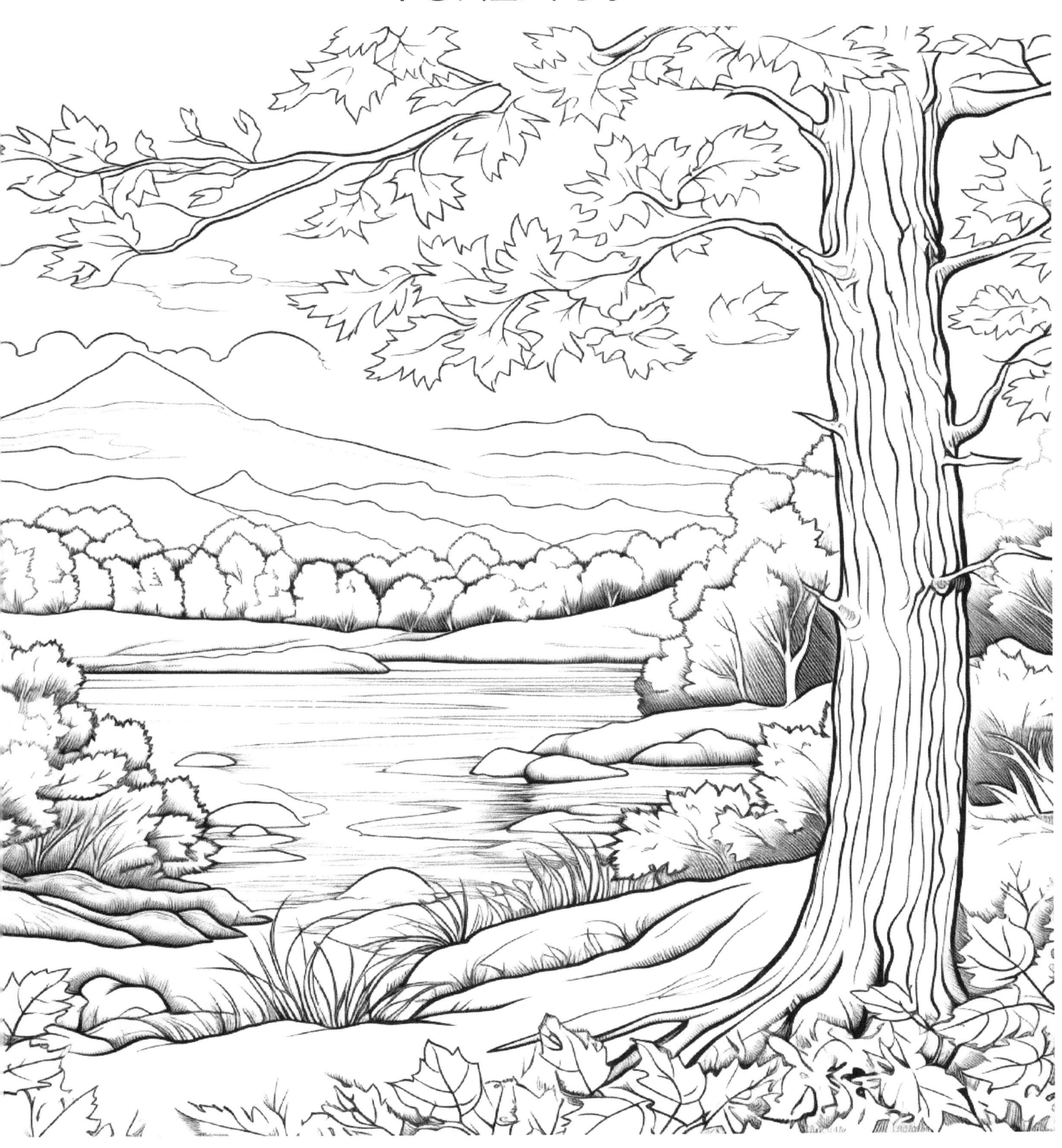

THE LORD YOUR GOD WILL
BE WITH YOU WHEREVER
YOU GO.
JOSHUA 1:9

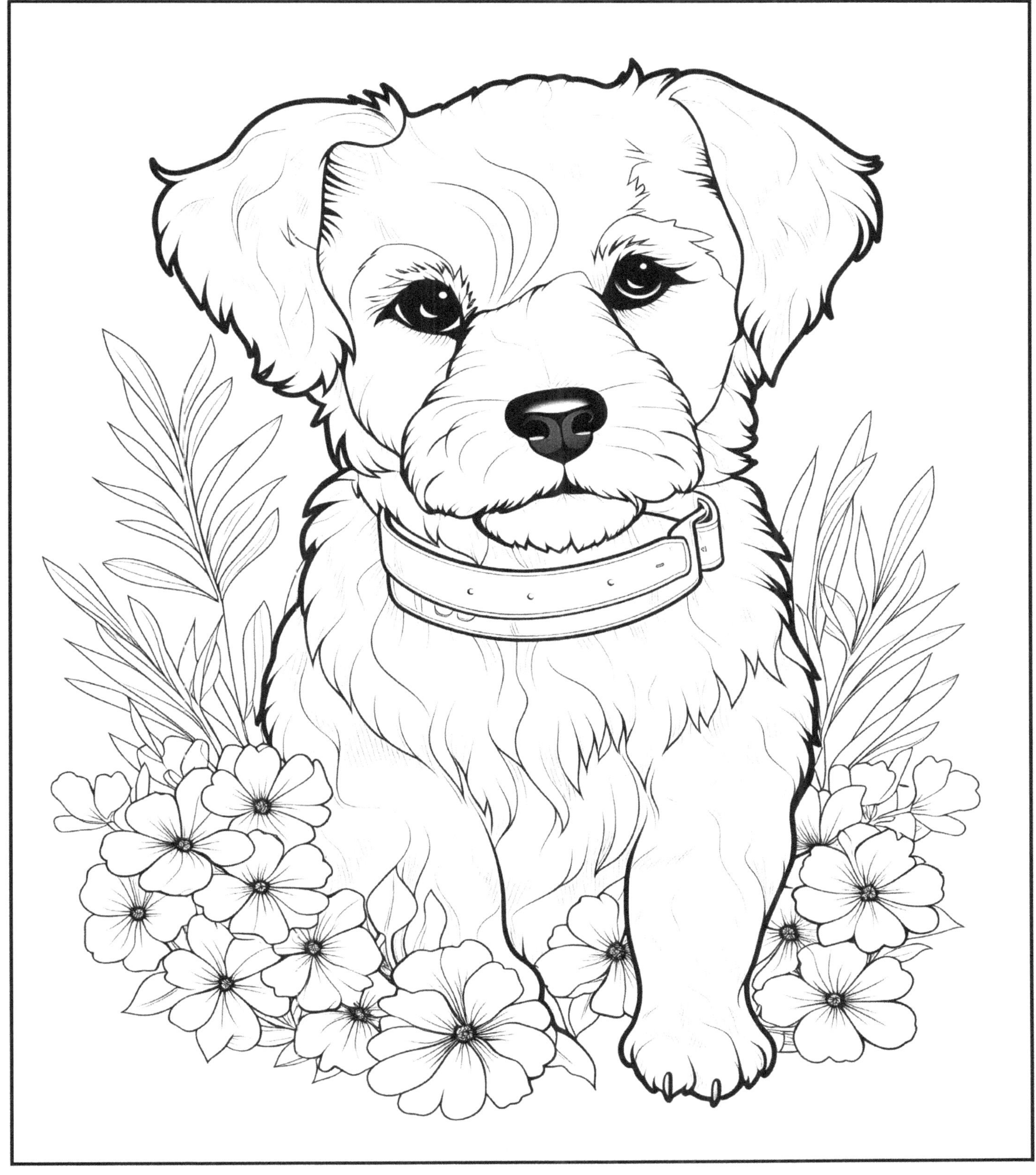

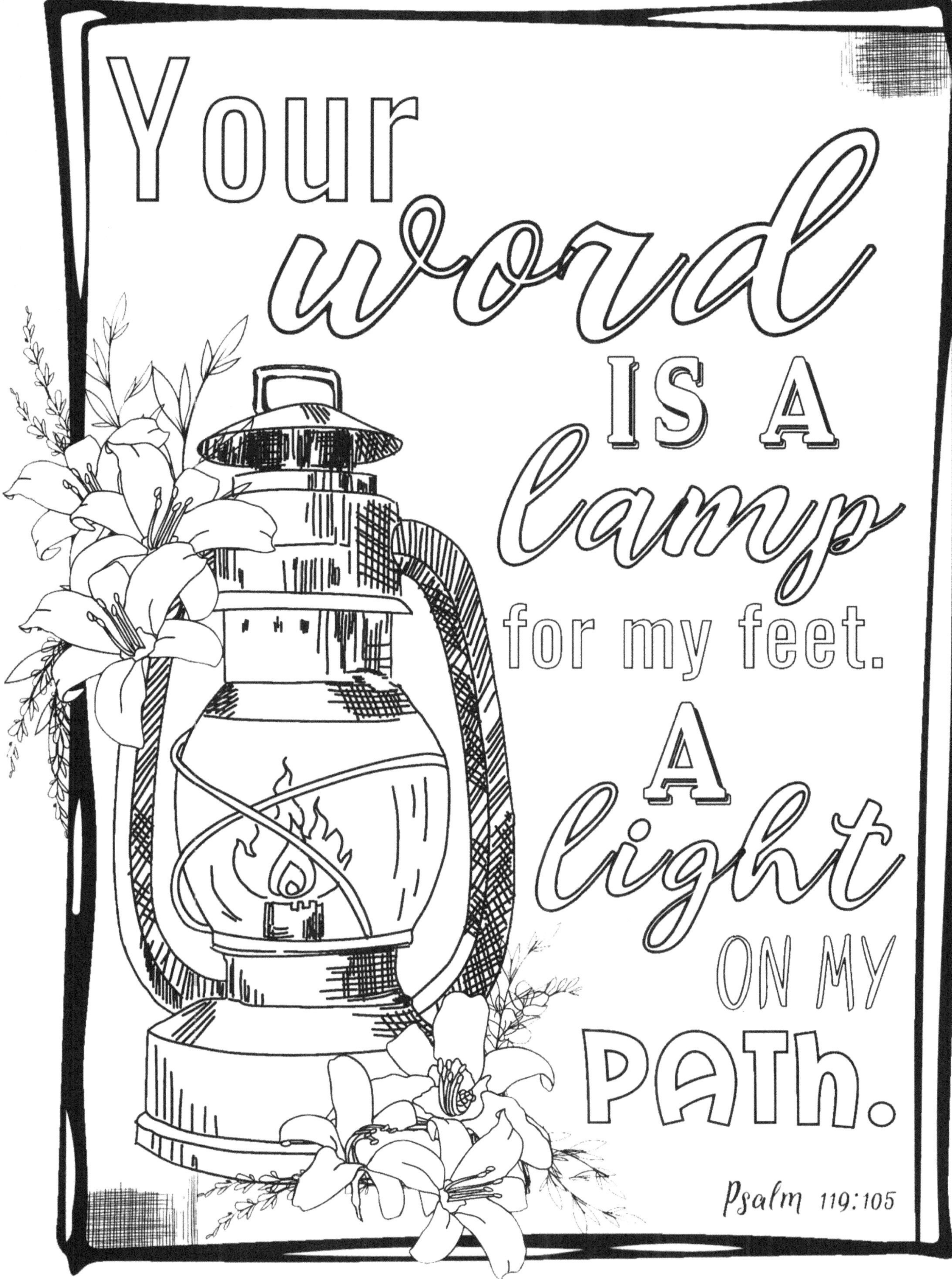

Your word is a lamp for my feet. A light on my path.
Psalm 119:105

GOD ACTS ON BEHALF OF THE ONE WHO WAITS FOR HIM.

ISAIAH 64:4

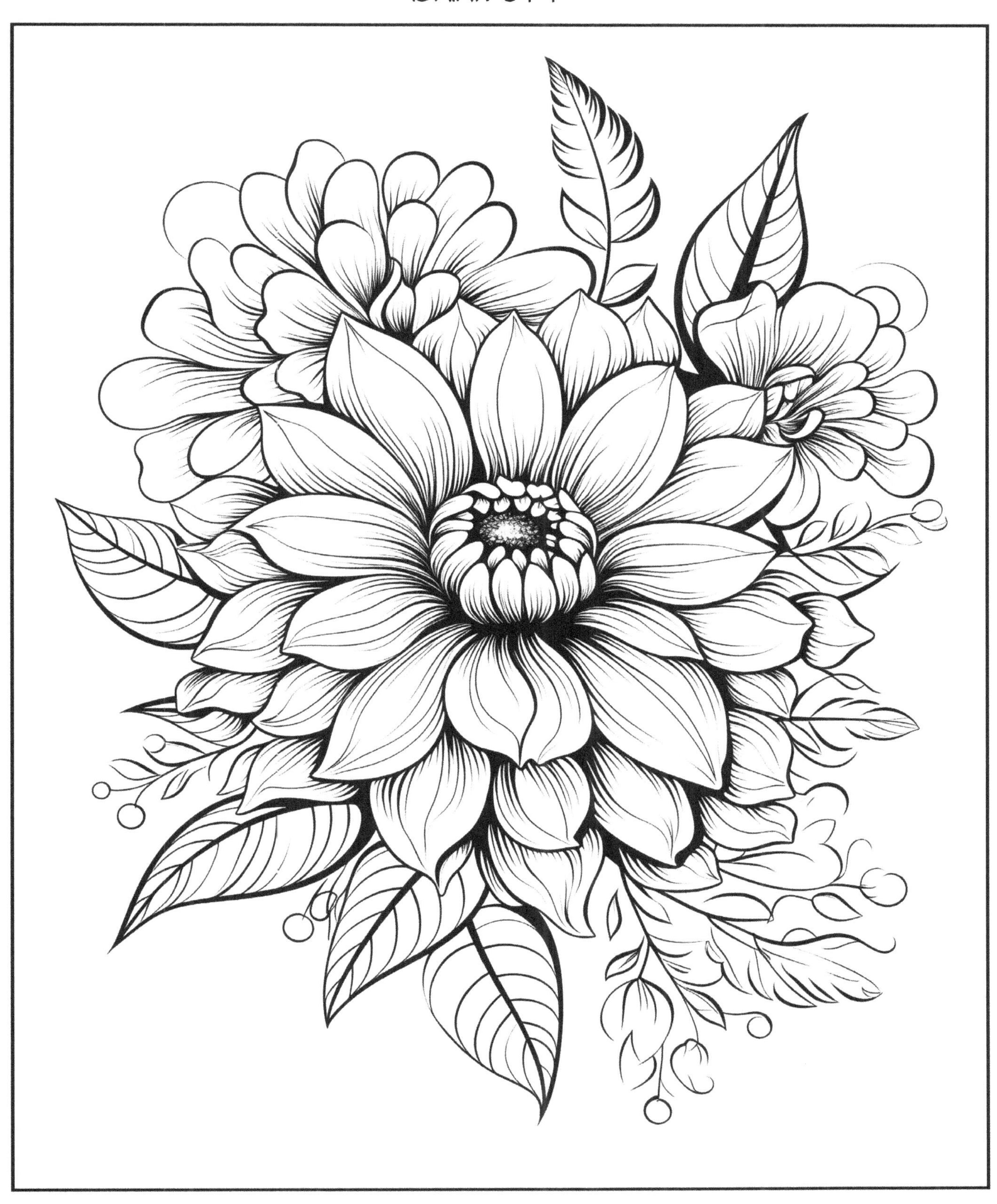

GOD ACTS ON BEHALF OF THE ONE WHO WAITS FOR HIM.

THE LORD WILL GIVE STRENGTH TO HIS PEOPLE. THE LORD WILL BLESS HIS PEOPLE WITH PEACE.

PSALM 29:11

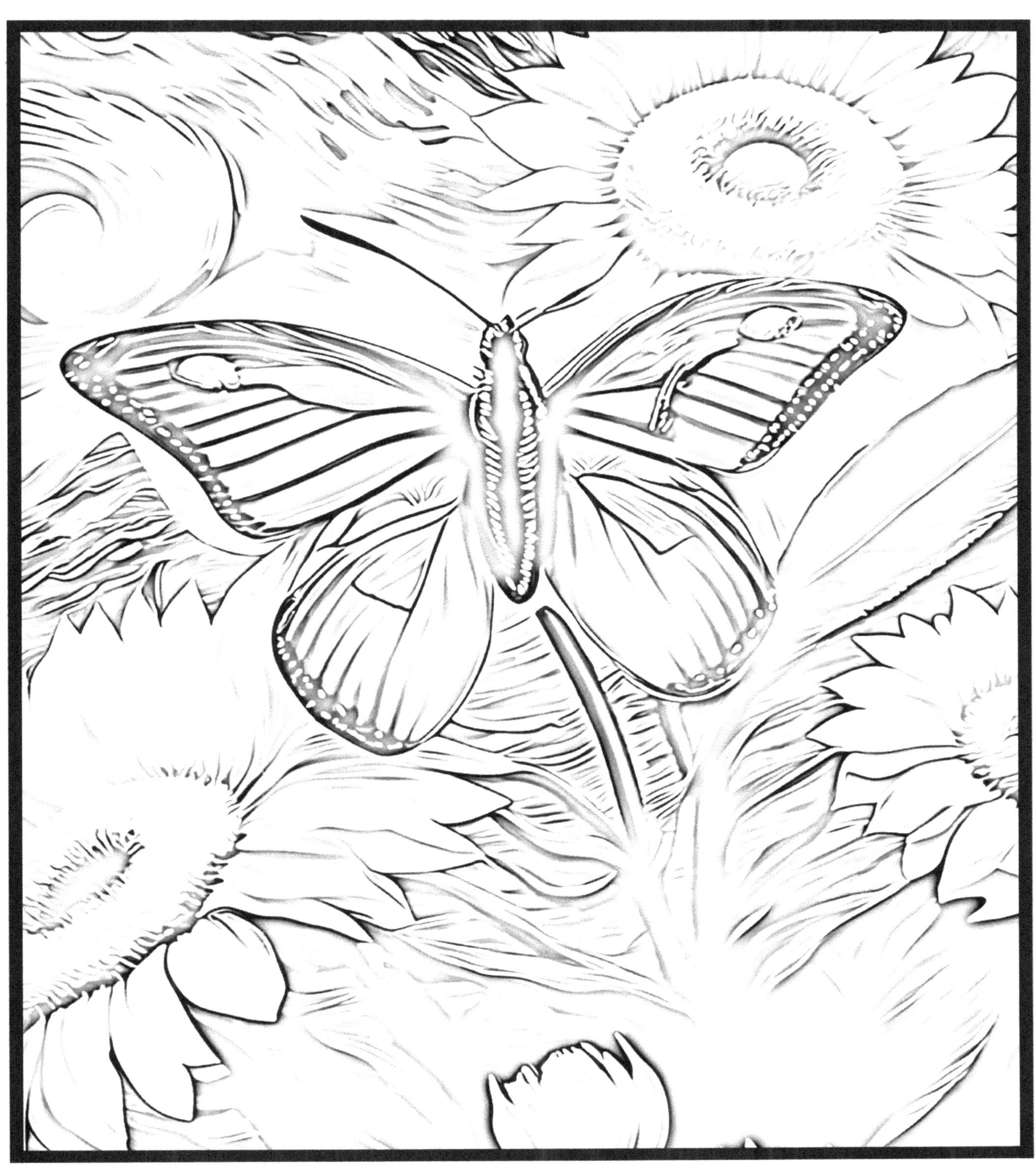

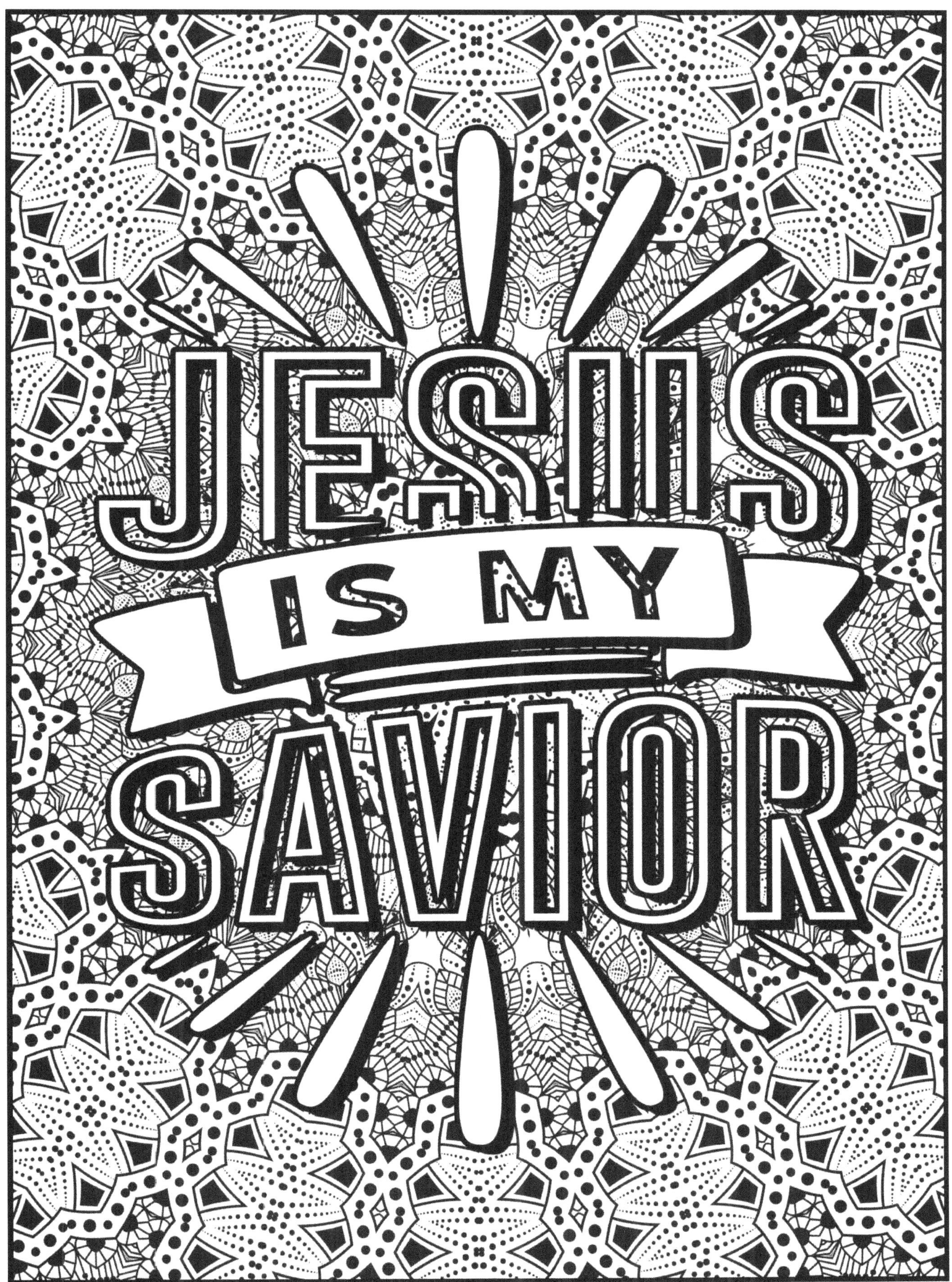

JESUS
IS MY
SAVIOR

THE LORD'S EYES MOVE TO AND FRO THROUGHOUT THE EARTH TO HELP THOSE WHO ARE LOYAL TO HIM

2 CHRONICLES 16:9

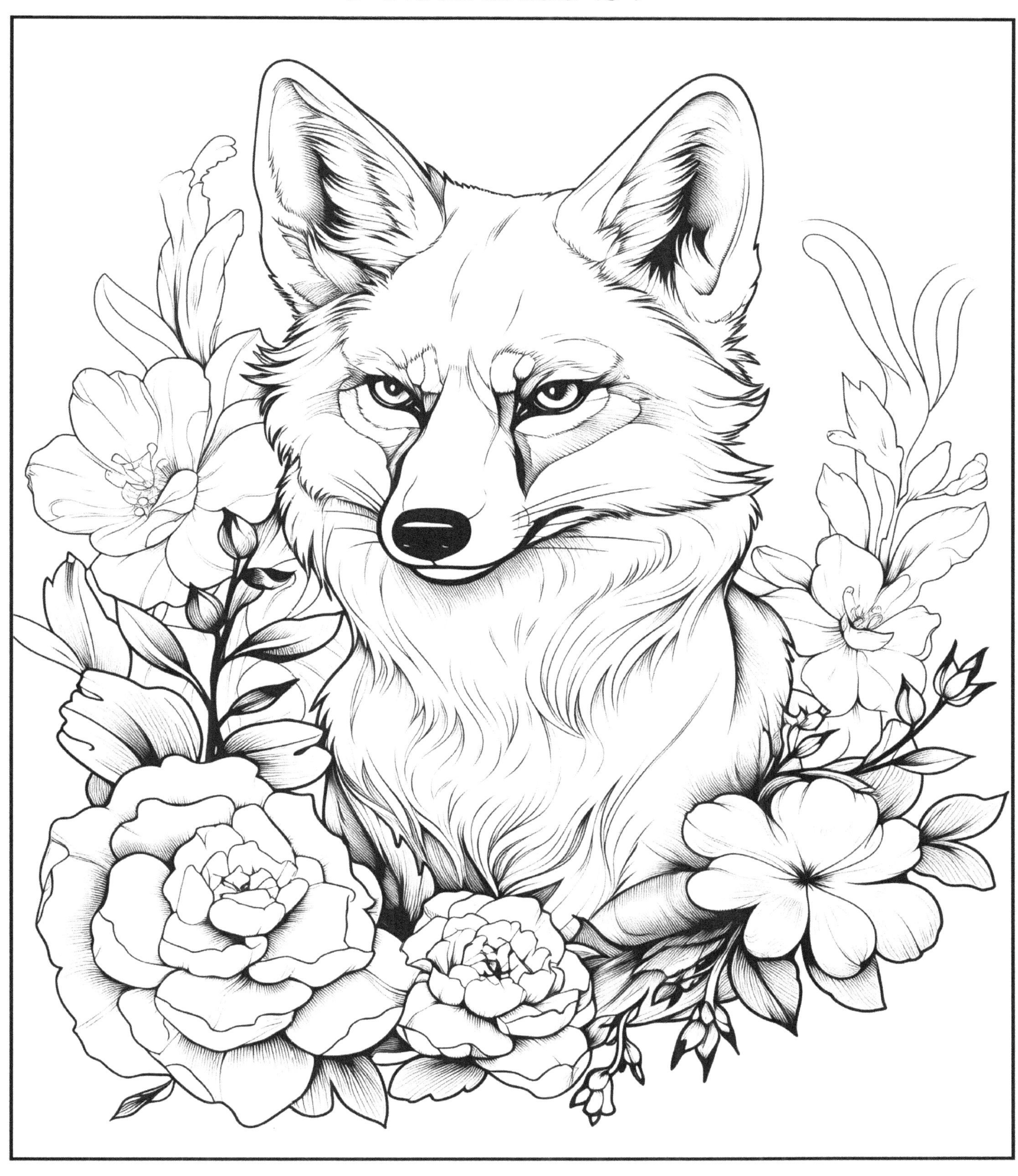

IF GOD CARES SO WONDERFULLY FOR THE WILDFLOWERS
...HE WILL CERTAINLY CARE FOR YOU

MATTHEW 6:30

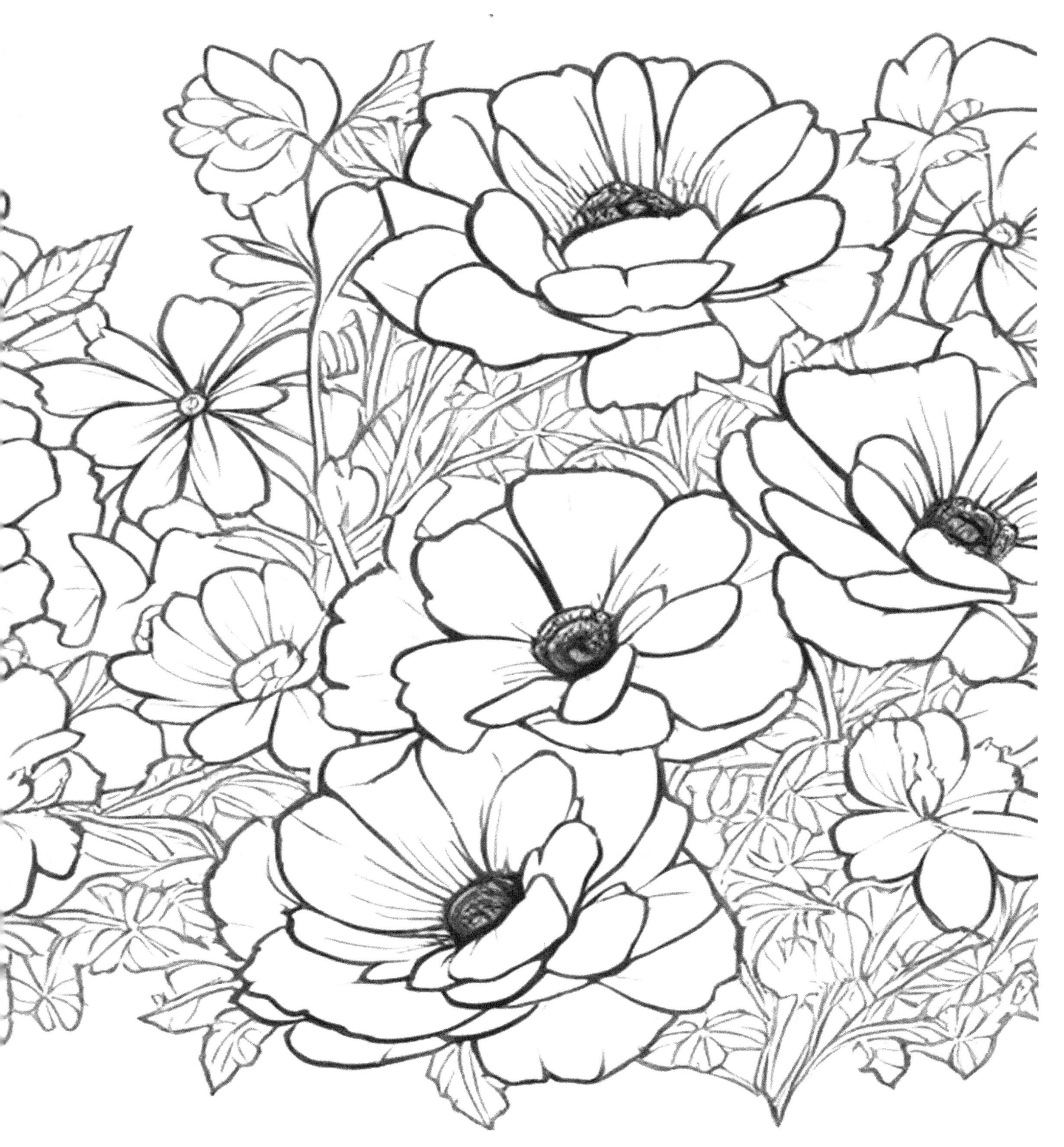

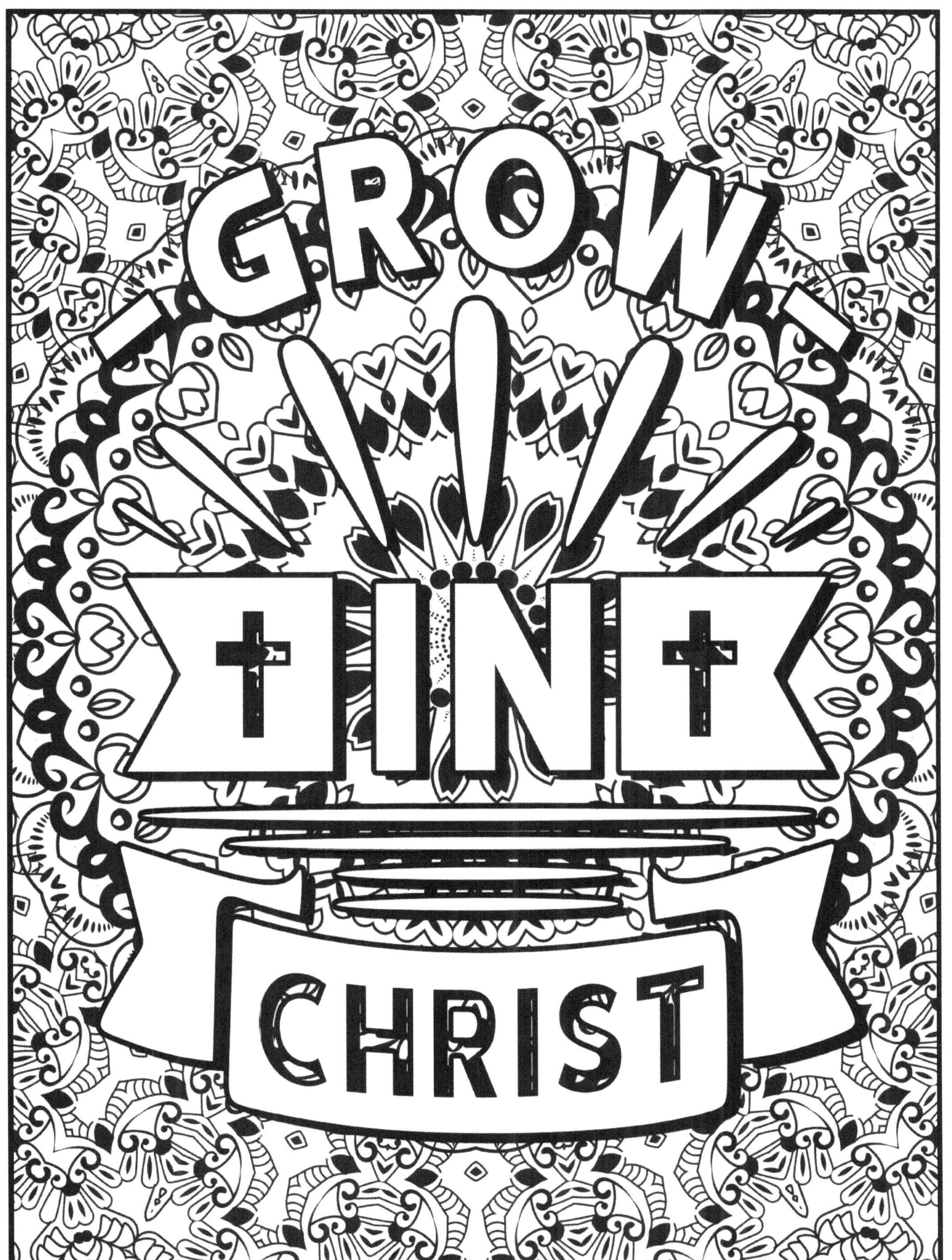
GROW
IN
CHRIST

CAST YOUR CARES ON THE LORD
AND HE WILL SUSTAIN YOU
PSALM 55:22

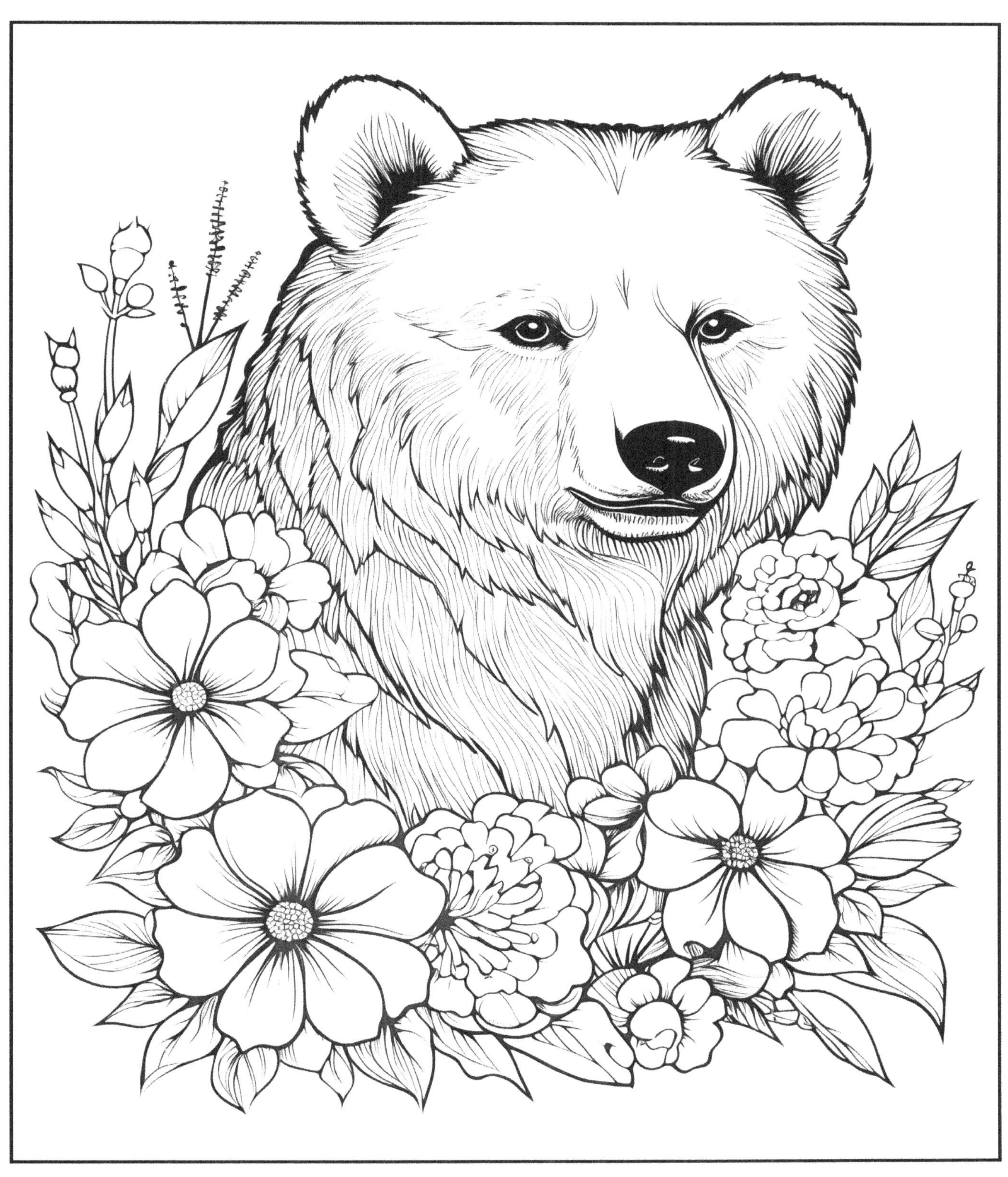

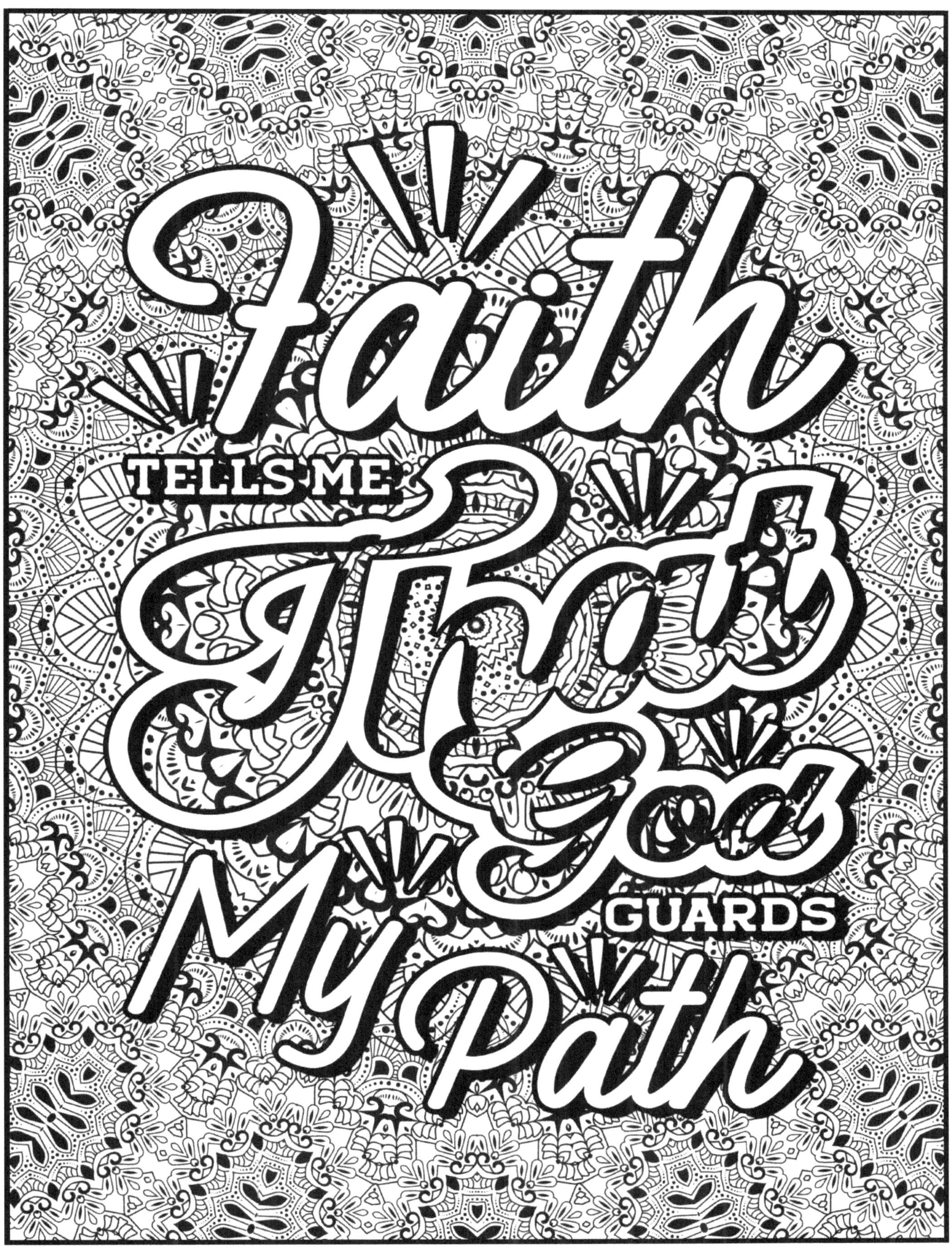
Faith
TELLS ME
That
God
GUARDS
My
Path

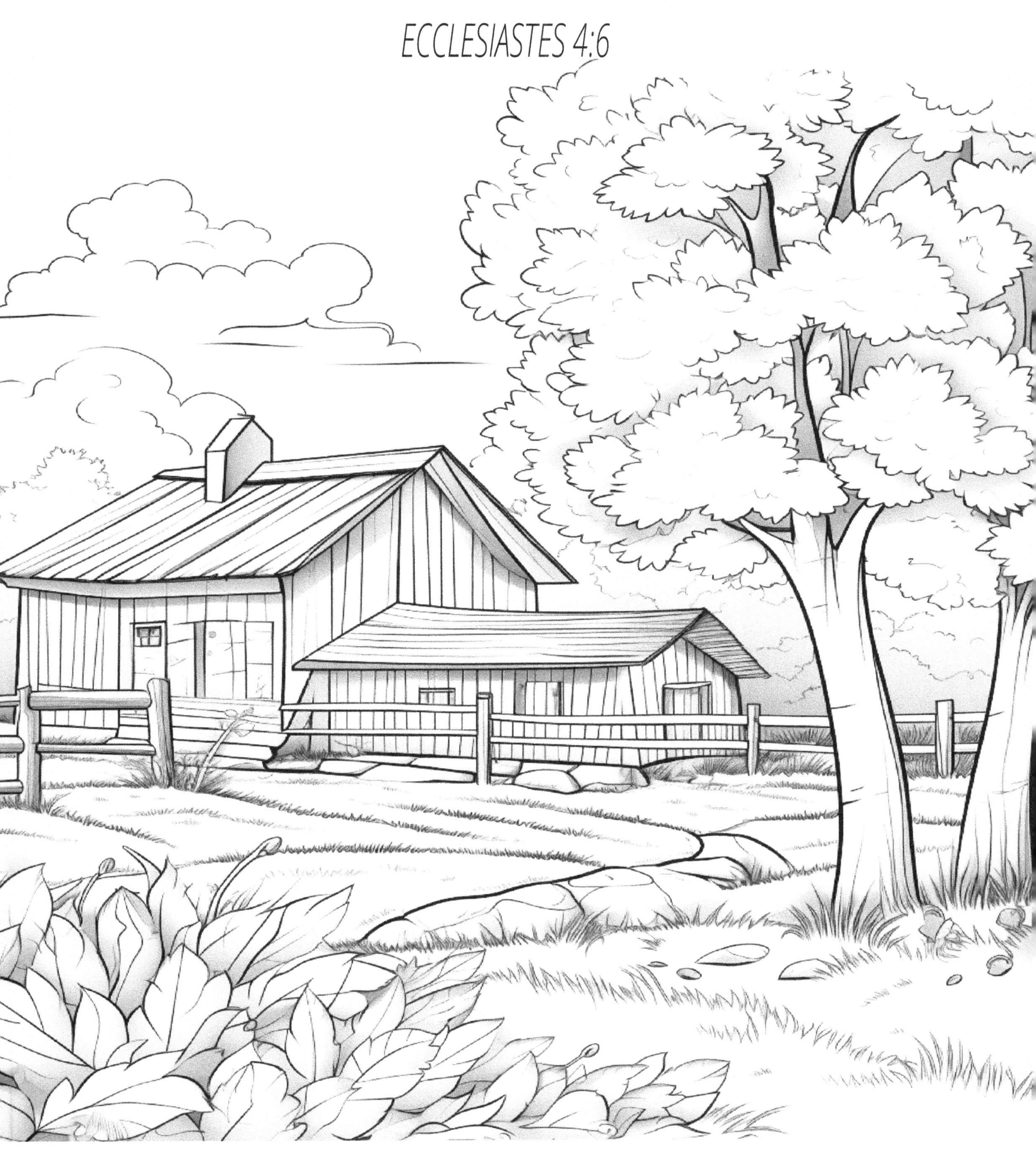

BETTER ONE HANDFUL WITH TRANQUILITY THAN TWO HANDFULS
CHASING AFTER THE WIND.
ECCLESIASTES 4:6

THE BLESSING OF THE LORD BRINGS WEALTH AND HE ADDS NO SORROW TO IT
PROVERBS 10:22

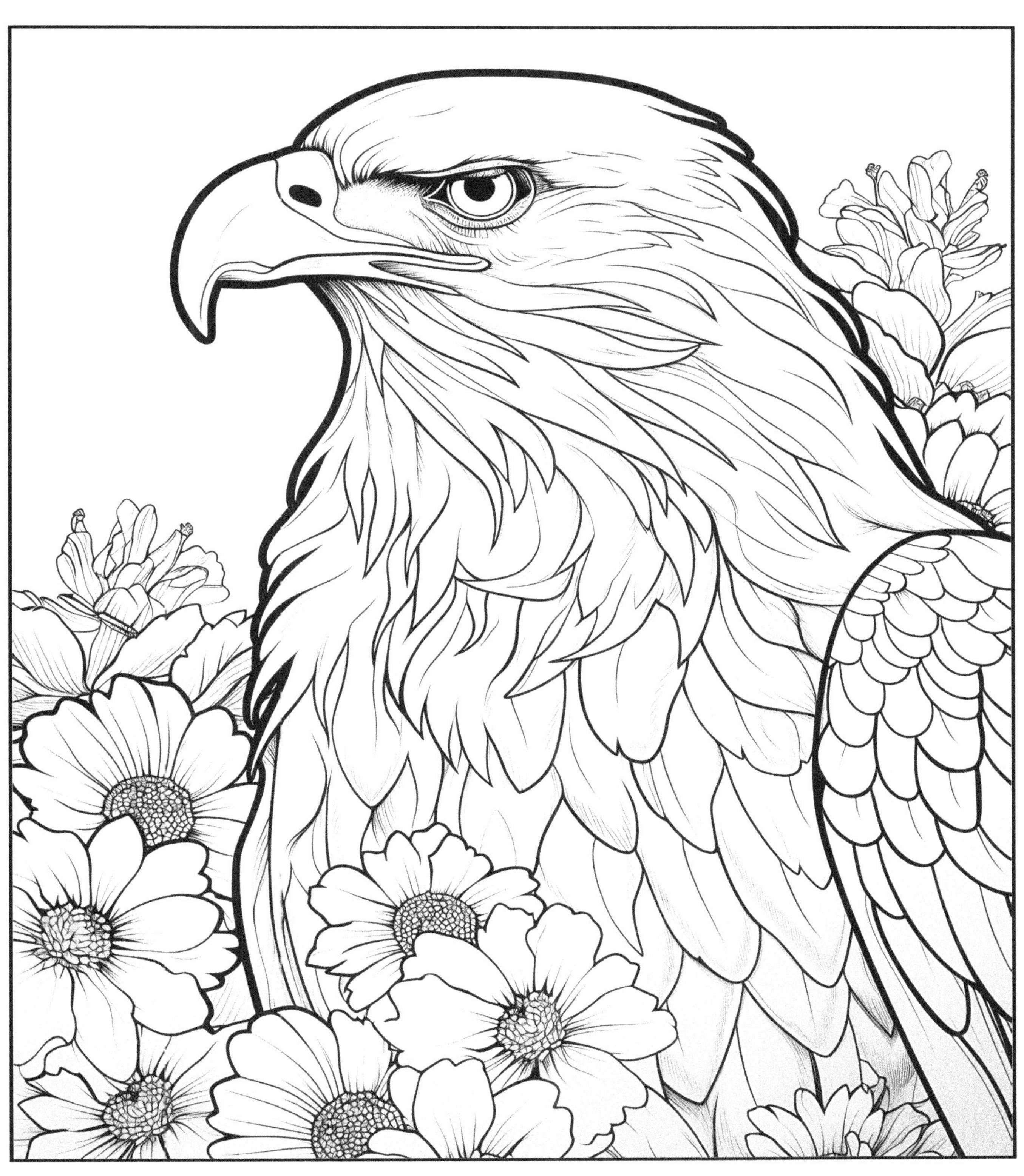

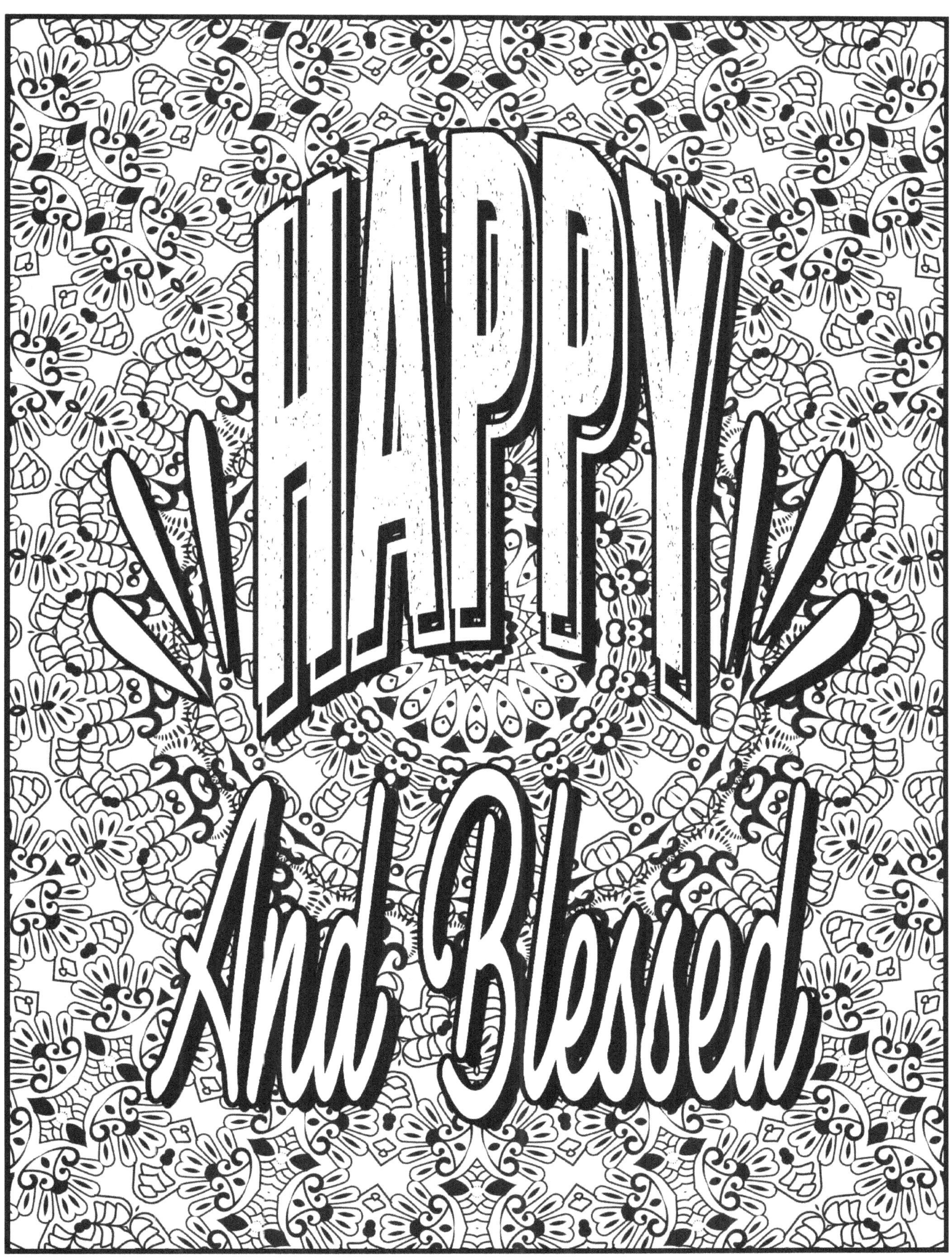

HAPPY
And Blessed

BE STRONG IN THE LORD AND THE POWER OF HIS MIGHT

EPHESIANS 6:10

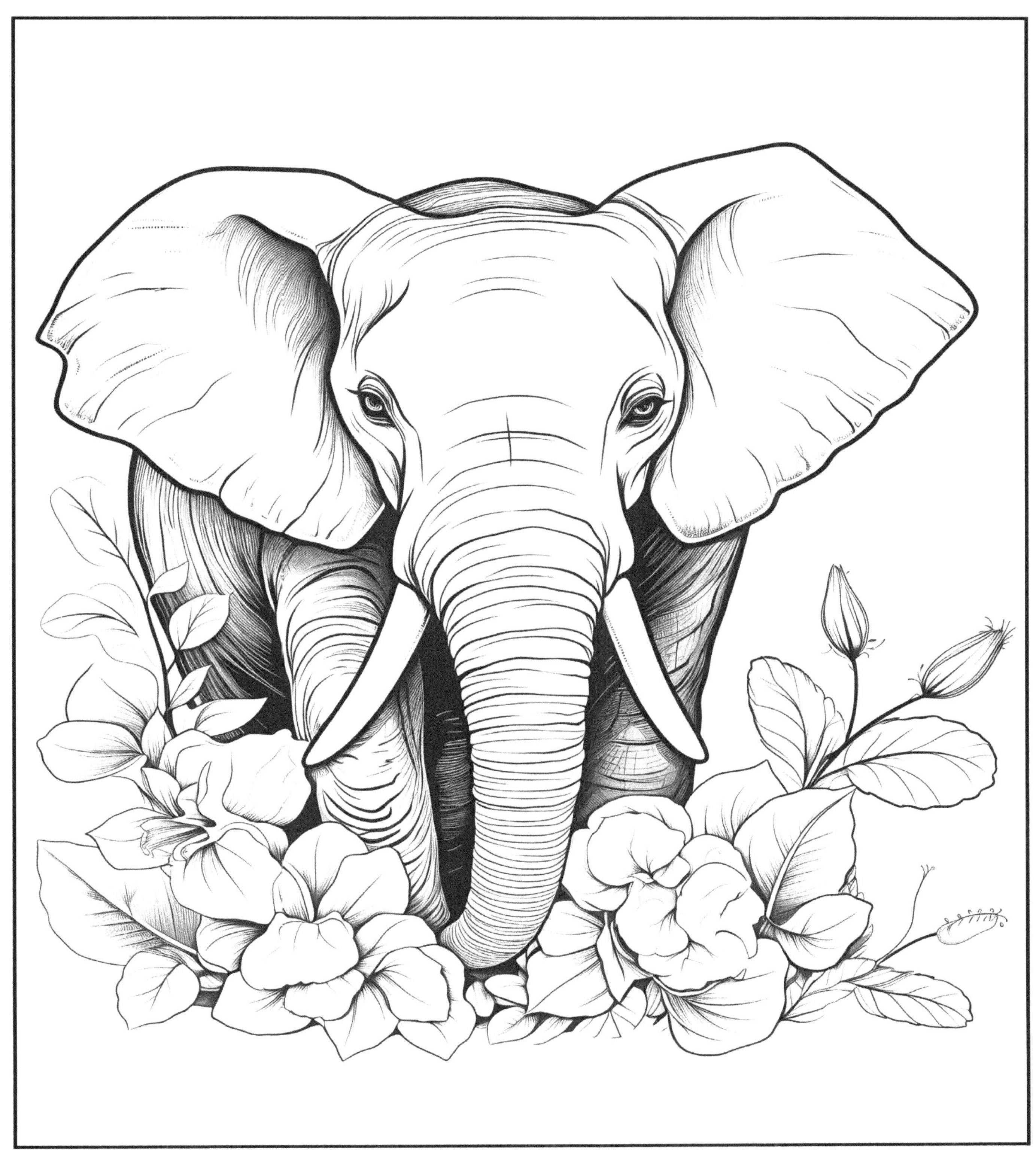

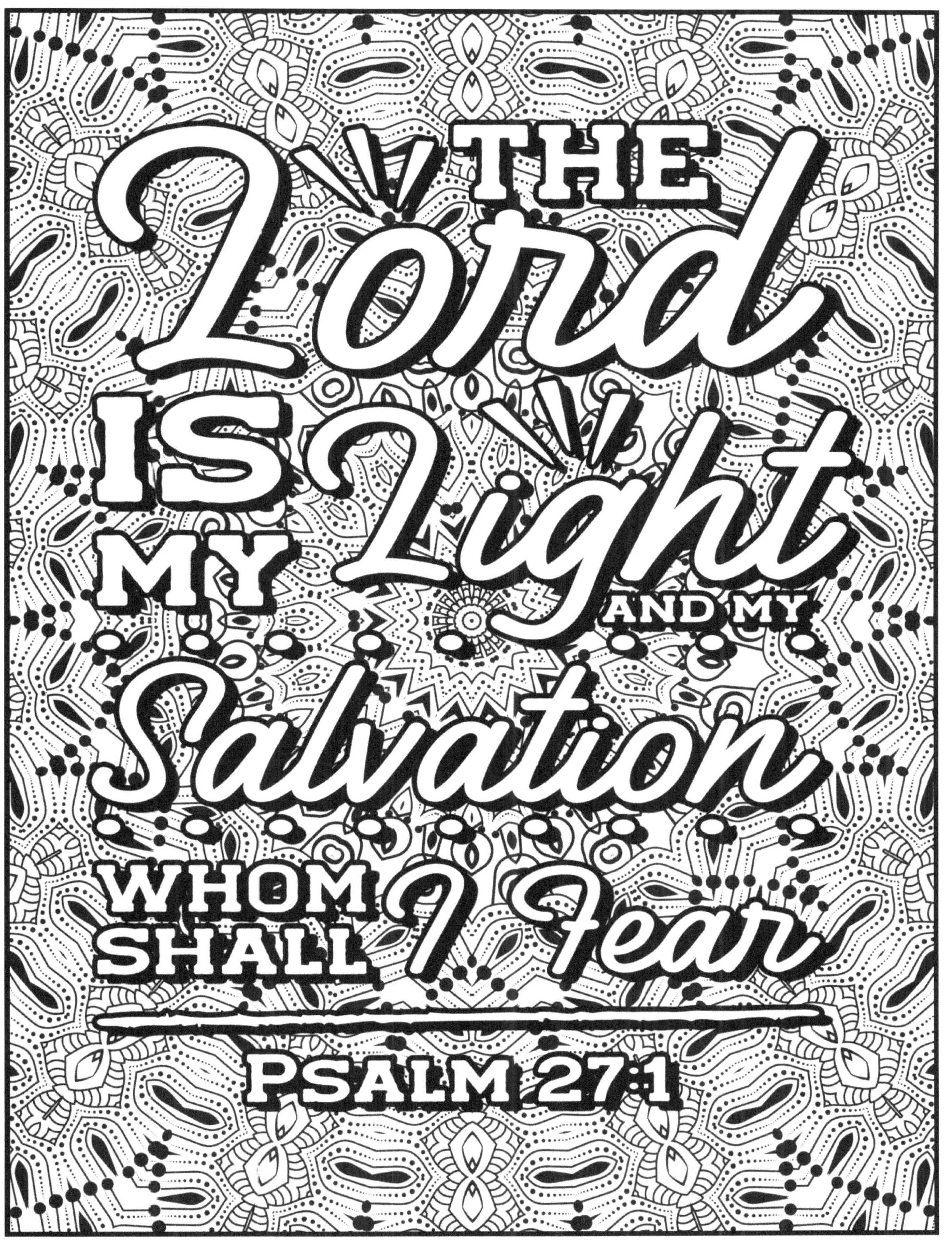

THE Lord IS MY Light AND MY Salvation WHOM SHALL I Fear
PSALM 27:1

BLESSED ARE THE HUMBLE

MATTHEW 5:5

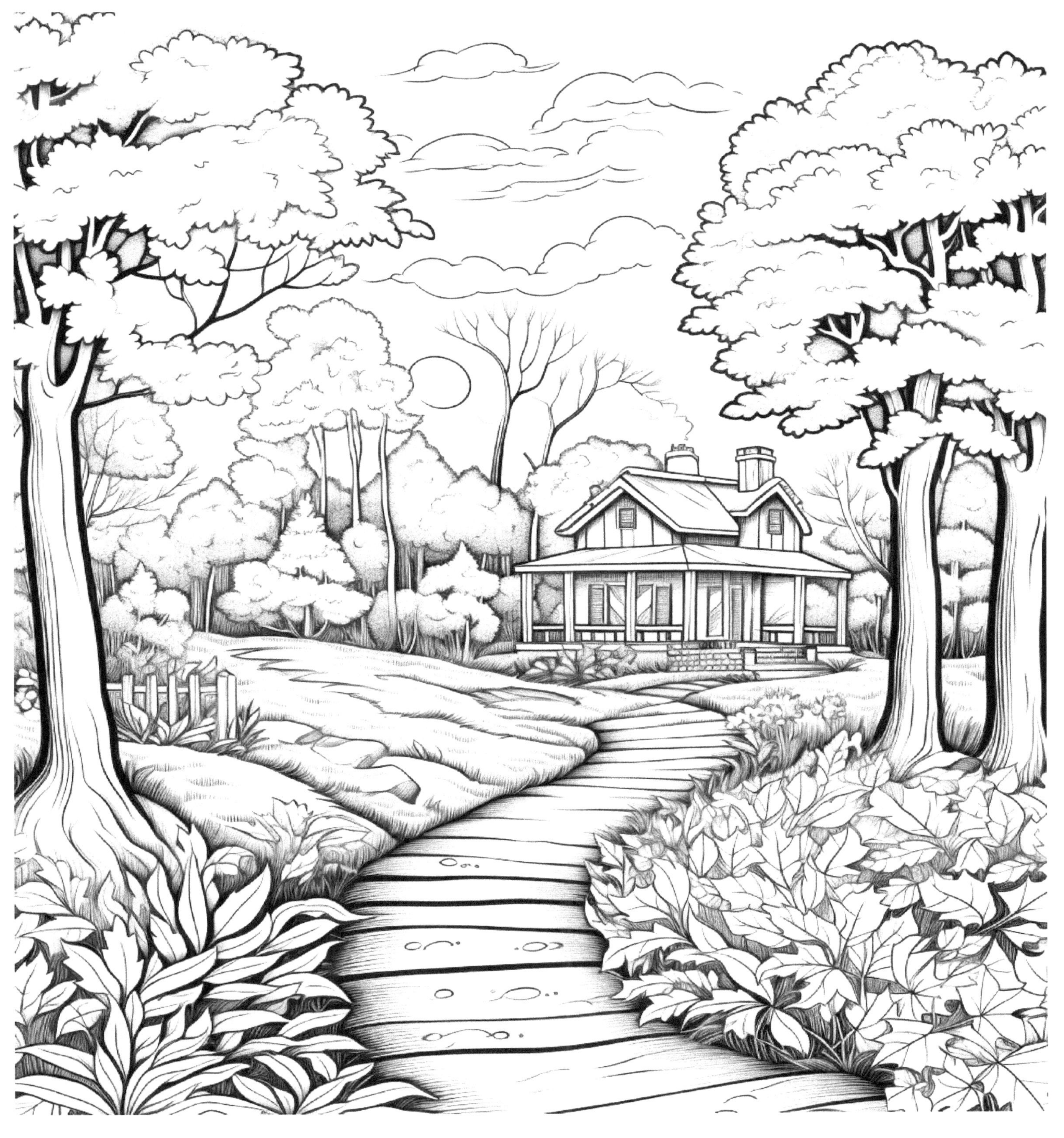

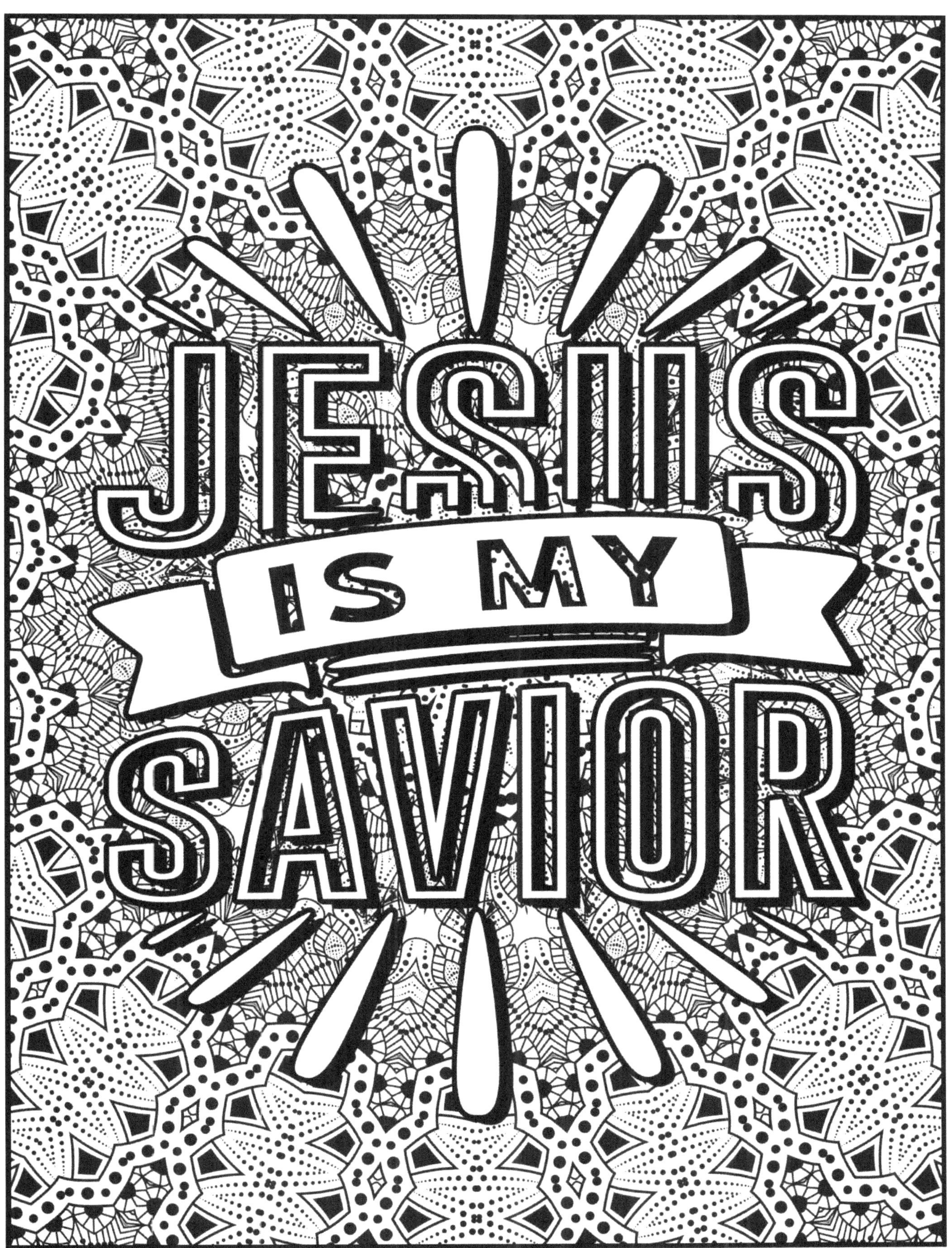

JESUS
IS MY
SAVIOR

THE GRASS WITHERS THE FLOWERS FADE, BUT THE WORD OF THE LORD WILL STAND FOREVER

ISAIAH 40:8

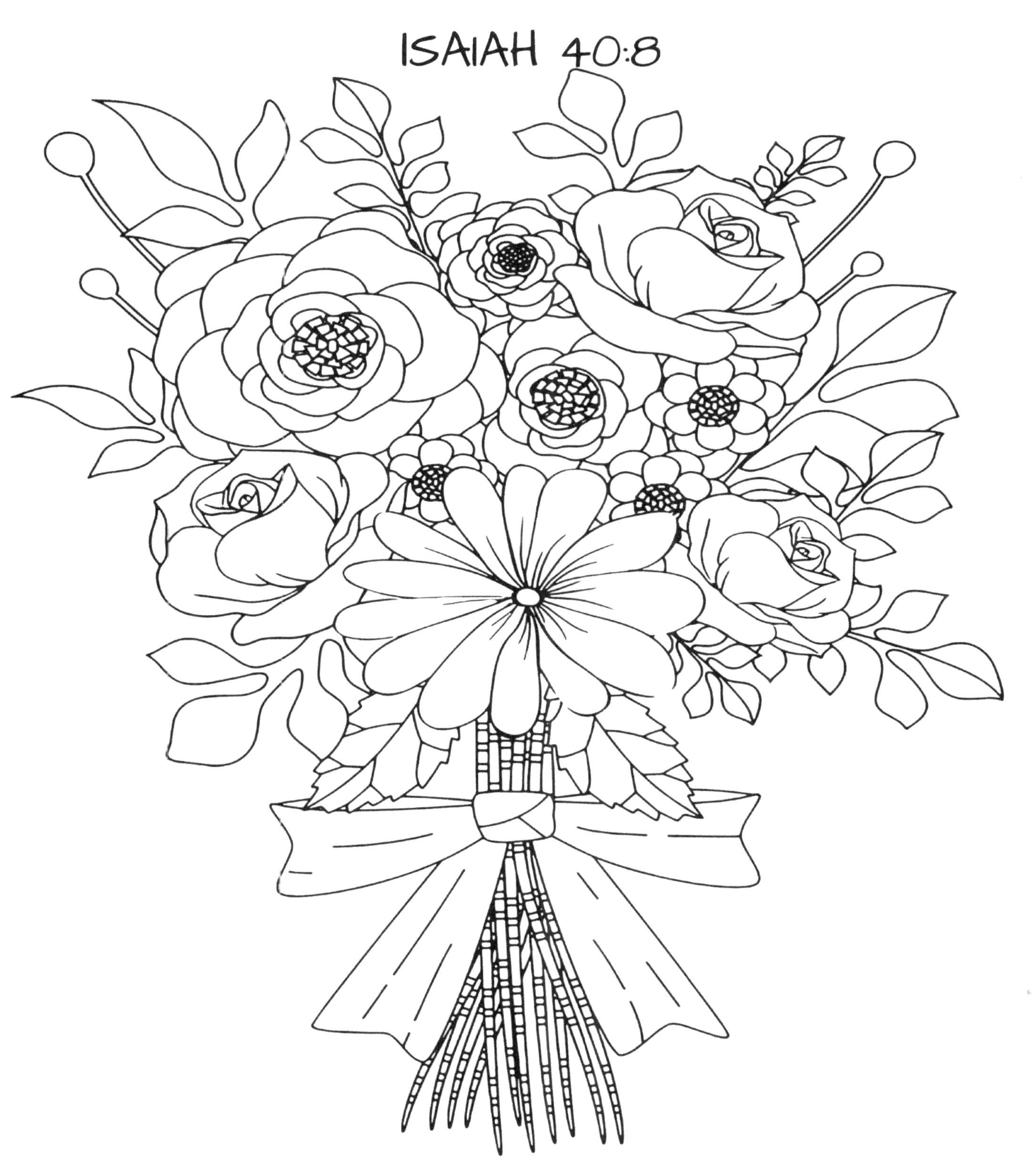

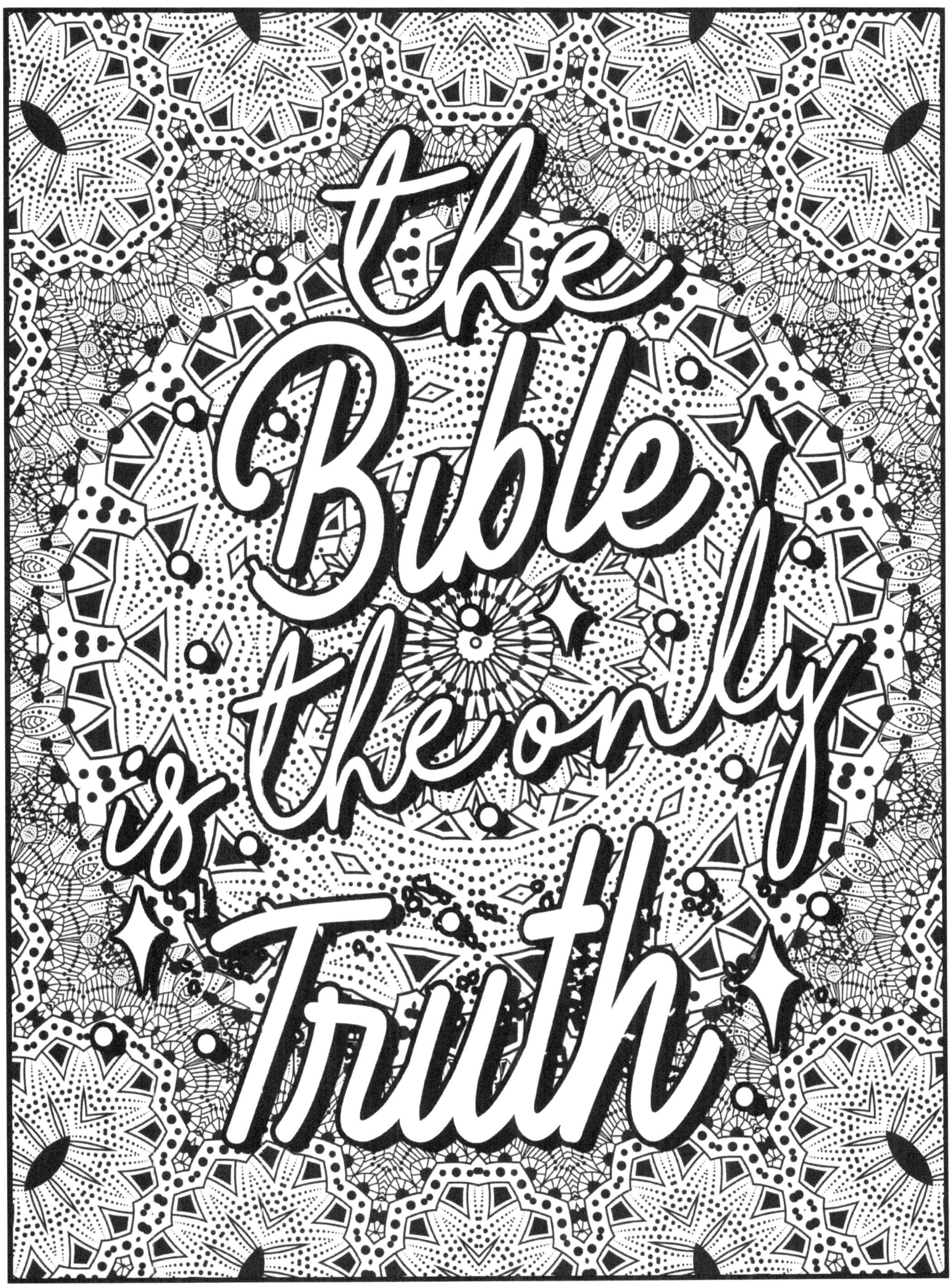

the Bible is the only Truth

FOR I KNOW THE PLANS I HAVE FOR YOU DECLARES THE LORD, PLANS FOR WELFARE AND NOT EVIL

JEREMIAH 29:11

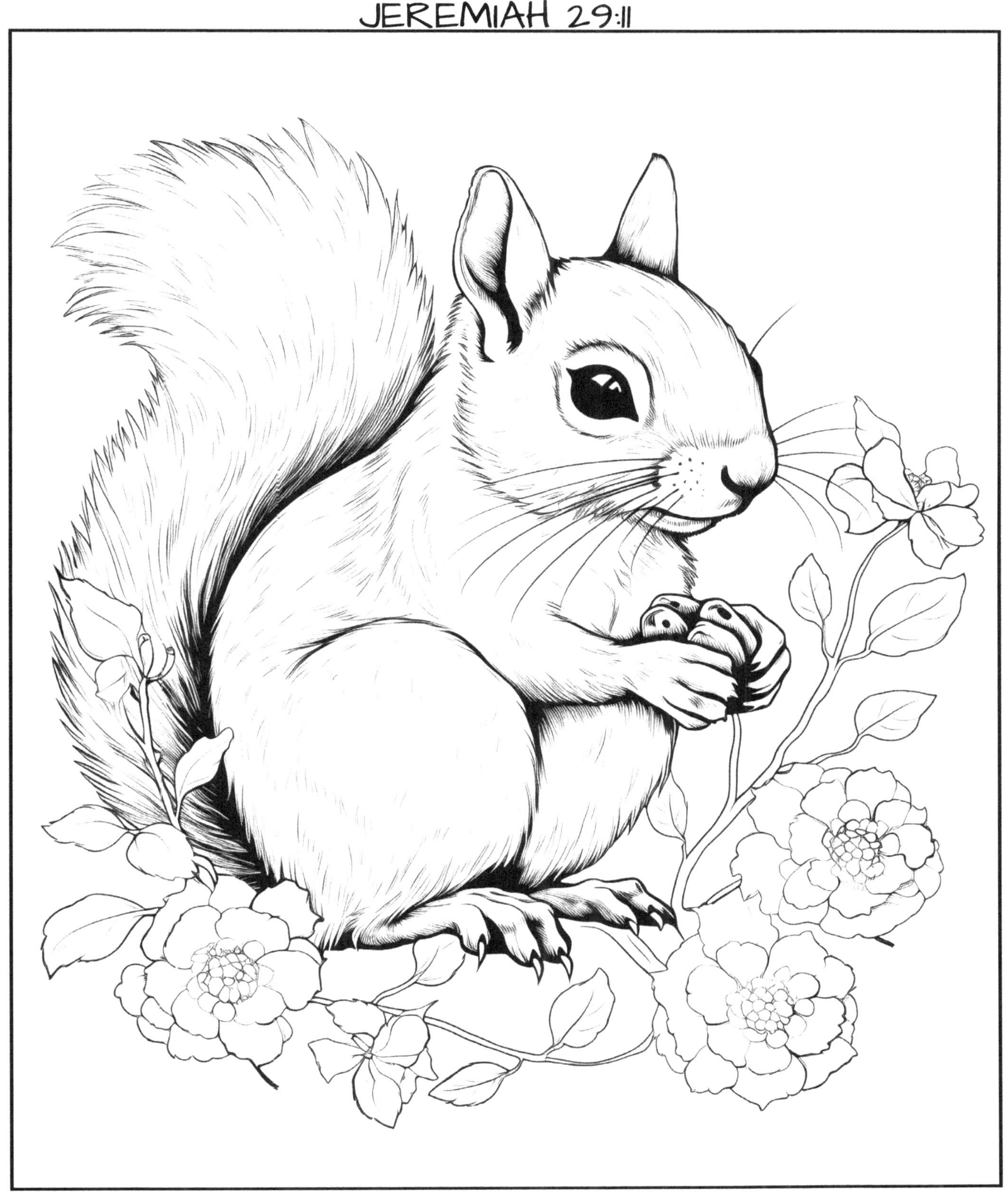

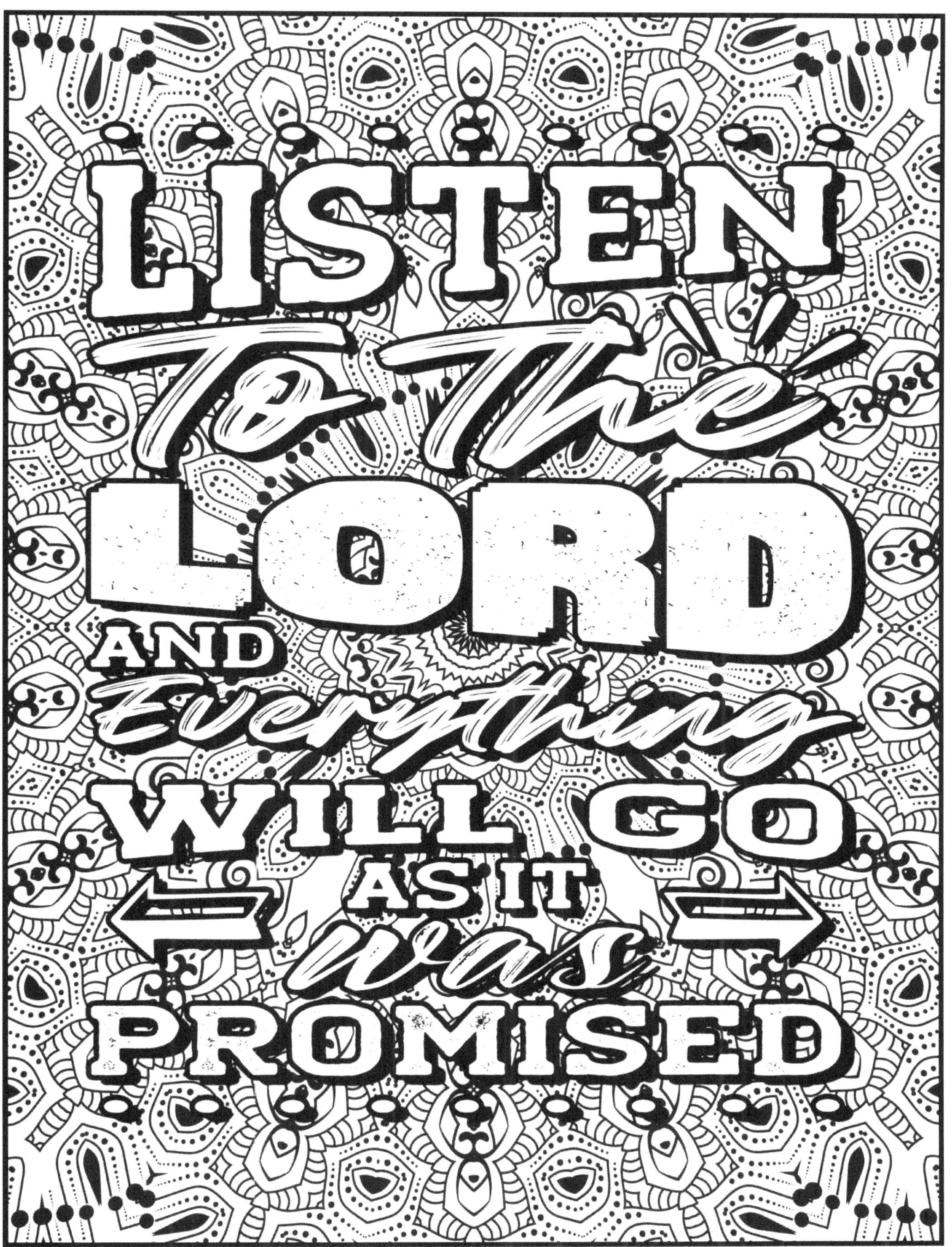

LISTEN
To The
LORD
AND
Everything
WILL GO
AS IT
Was
PROMISED

PRAYER OF SALVATION:

Lord Jesus,
I choose to
turn from my life of sin.
I ask that you come into my heart,
so I can follow you as my Lord and
my Savior
Amen

For God So Loved The World
That He Gave His Only Begotten
Son
That Whosoever Believes In Him
Shall Not Perish
BUT SHALL HAVE ETERNAL
LIFE
John 3:16

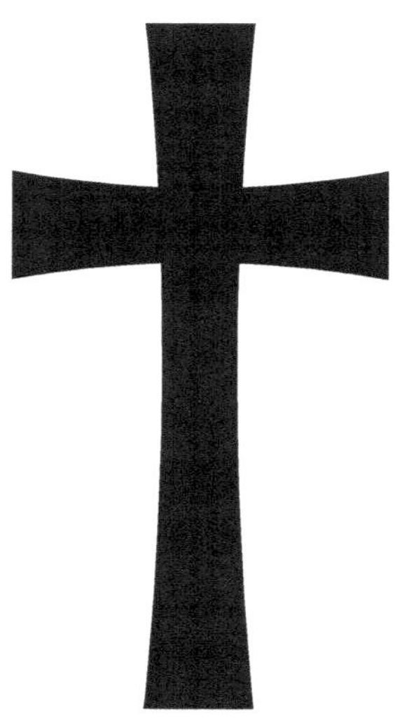